Kidnapped by the Celtic King

The spring rains fell lightly on the farm of Calpornius and Conchesa. It was almost time to begin planting. Patricius was looking forward to doing something other than his regular farm chores and sheep tending. No one in their tiny family could believe how fast the days were going by. It hardly seemed possible that they were already quite far into the year 405.

Calpornius had just finished breakfast and was beginning to put on his official white robes. He had a town council meeting to attend and would need to leave his farm for a day or two. As soon as Patricius had finished saddling his father's horse, he said, "Don't worry, Father, I will take good care of the farm while you are away. After all, I am almost sixteen years old."

"I am not so concerned about the farm, Son, as I am about you and your mother," said Calpornius. After several moments the wind began to blow in from the sea and a salty mist could be felt in the air. Calpornius added, "The Irish raiders are becoming more bold every month, and I fear that they may attack our farm while I am away. Be sure you keep a sharp eye on the sea, my son, and don't go wandering off without your sword."

"Yes, yes, Father," said Patricius impatiently.

After Calpornius had given his final instructions to his servants and kissed his wife farewell, he mounted his horse and slowly trotted away. As he began to distance himself from his farm and family, a strange feeling began to weigh down his spirit. It was as if he could sense that danger or tragedy was soon to appear, but he did not know where or when it would arise. A few moments later, Calpornius stopped his horse and turned around to see his wife and son waving to him in the distance. As this concerned father hesitated for a moment, he began to pray for his family. He prayed, "Lord, please watch over my family and do what is best for them."

Despite his concern for his family, Calpornius realized that he must press on with his duties at the council meeting. He turned his horse, therefore, onto the road once again and proceeded toward the town at a quick pace.

Patricius watched his father disappear over the horizon, then turned to his mother and asked, "Mother, what would you like me to do this morning? I could finish some of the school work that Father and my tutor Julius left for me, or I could inspect our flock of sheep in the north pasture."

Conchesa replied, "You are the man of the house now, my son. You make up your own mind and do what you think would please God and your father."

"Very well," said Patricius, "I think that I will go pay a visit to the shepherd and see how our flocks are getting on before I pick up my studies."

Several minutes later, Patricius began to walk a mile or so to where his father's servant was caring for a large flock of sheep. It was almost time to sheer the sheep, and that was one chore he really liked. Patricius ran through his father's apple orchard and through the pasture to where the sheep were grazing.

"Well, if it isn't the master's son himself," said the old shepherd. "What brings you out to the field today?"

Patricius gazed at the frightened sheep for a moment and responded, "You would think these silly sheep would know me by now, why must they run away?"

"I guess they just like the sound of the shepherd's voice," said the servant, "besides, you do not come out to see them as much as you used to."

"My father wants me to spend more time in my studies," sighed Patricius, "I don't understand why learning math and language is so important!"

"Some day you will thank your father for forcing you to get an education," said the wise servant quietly.

"Their wool looks good," Patricius observed as he endeavored to change the subject. "When do you think we can take the wool coats off these creatures?"

"Soon," said the shepherd, "perhaps in a week or so. Your father will be pleased with the quality of the wool this season."

They were silent for a moment and then the young teenager remarked, "It is strangely quiet today...so quiet you can hear the gulls out beyond the shore."

"Yes it is rather odd," the old servant said in reply. "Their cries seldom carry this far unless they are chasing a vessel."

"I know," said Patricius nodding thoughtfully. Seconds later, his expression changed from puzzled to apprehensive. "Those gulls are trying to tell us something!" he exclaimed. "My father warned me about danger from the sea, I hope any ships coming our way are filled with Roman soldiers. They are strong enough to protect us from the Irish pirates."

"The Roman emperor is through sending us any soldiers," the shepherd said grimly. "Maybe that is for the best. We will have to learn to protect ourselves sooner or later, and then perhaps we will be strong enough to throw the Romans out. It will be great to be our own masters once more."

Patricius barely heard a word that the old shepherd told him. He was busy listening to the gulls once again. It was clearer than ever, to the young boy, that the birds must be excited about something important. "I'm going to the cliffs to see why they are making so much noise," he said.

"May the good Lord protect us all," the old servant responded, smiling.

As Patricius hurried toward the cliffs, his soft sandals clung to the smooth rocks for he was as much at home on the cliffs as a fish in the water. He soon reached the

top of the cliffs and looked out over the cold, grey sea. Sometimes it was possible to see the coastline of Ireland across the North Channel which separated the two lands. On that particular day, however, the clouds were so thick that he could not see the distant shores of Ireland.

A few moments later, Patricius heard the sounds of splashing water. He lowered his eyes to the white beach below. Normally, the beach near his home was deserted except, perhaps, for a fisherman's boat. But not today, for as the young lad gazed down he saw many large boats filled with strong men who were heavily armed. Some of the boats had already landed. Others, rowed by at least twenty men, were speeding toward the shore. Patricius had never seen anything like this in his whole life. Were these soldiers friend or foe? The young teenager was anxious to find out the answer to that question!

The familiar gulls were hovering low now, crying perhaps for food. They knew that fishermen in boats usually threw out a few small fish to the birds—but these men had no fish in their boats. They were not fishermen. Stranger still, they had long streaming hair and carried crude shields and spears.

At first, Patricius thought that the new comers were Roman soldiers. Then he noticed, however, that these men were not wearing the armor or uniform of Roman soldiers. Suddenly, the young teenager began to fear that these soldiers were nothing more than raiders who were bent on plundering the coastal farms and villages of Roman Britain.

As soon as all of the soldiers had landed, they began to assemble on the beach. The shouts of the men could barely be heard in the still air. What were they saying? It was a strange language that Patricius had never heard. He decided to climb down the cliff far enough to get a better idea of who these men really were.

The cliff rose two hundred feet above the beach. In some places, it was a sheer drop, but Patricius had often climbed this cliff. He felt certain that he could get halfway down it without being discovered by the men on the beach, so he started to descend cautiously. The rock of the cliff was gray and white, but here and there it was spotted with small purple flowers. If the men below looked up, they would not notice him, he thought. His purple tunic would blend into the colors of the cliff.

Here and there, sturdy shrubs and small trees had somehow found places among the crevices of the cliff to grow strong roots. Patricius hung onto the shrubs, and with his outstretched feet, he carefully felt for a place to stand. Slowly he inched his way down the cliff. Once, a shrub pulled away when he hung from it, and his heart almost stopped beating as a shower of dirt and small stones rained down on the men below. But they were too busy unloading their boats to notice.

Halfway down the cliff, Patricius rested on a small ledge. The rest of the descent would be easy, because at that point the cliff sloped gently toward the beach. Patricius lay on the floor of the ledge and listened to the loud talk of the men below. As he studied their clothing, he suddenly realized with horror that these were indeed the forces of one of the Celtic Sea Kings. His father had often spoken about them and had even described their harsh speech. Fear clutched at the young man's heart. These were no Roman soldiers—these were Celtic raiders looking for plunder.

They were all assembled on the beach now. Their leader, a huge man, held up a hand for silence. In his other hand, he carried a long, crude-looking spear, and slung over his shoulder was a bright red shield. He spoke briefly to his men and then pointed inland, shouting "Bannavem!" The others took up the cry, "Bannavem!"

A chill went down Patricius's spine.

Bannavem was the name of the village only four miles inland where his father was now sitting with the other members of the council. Bannavem was also the place where his mother had eventually decided to spend the day shopping. For this reason, Patricius knew that he had to warn the townspeople that raiders were on the way, or everyone in town would fall victim to the ruthless warriors. Patricius had to get to Bannavem before the raiders. If he could climb back to the top of the cliff, he would have only two miles to travel to the town.

The raiders were starting to march along the beach and Patricius figured that they would take the long way around the cliff. It would take them nearly an hour to reach the town. With effort he could make it in half that time. He drew a deep breath and then turned to begin the upward climb.

He reached for a small tree to help draw himself up a few steps. For a moment, all of his weight was pulling on the little tree, then disaster struck! The roots of the tree were not deeply embedded in the crevices of the cliff, and Patricius suddenly pulled the tree, roots and all, out of its shallow anchoring. Clawing the air, he fell backward. As he tumbled down the cliff, he tried desperately to grab at bushes, shrubs, and jagged rocks, but in vain. He tumbled head over heals down the steep slope, bringing rocks and

dirt with him.

    Suddenly, Patricius saw a bright explosion, as though a bolt of lightning had split the sky. His head had hit a rock and he had been knocked unconscious. His body rolled limply the rest of the way and came to a stop in front of King Nial, the leader of the raiders.

"These British can't wait for us to take them," the sea king bellowed with laughter. "They insist upon coming to us." He turned the unconscious boy over and looked down at him. "A fine sturdy lad," he said putting his head to the boy's chest to feel his heartbeat, then nodding.

"A tumble like that is nothing to a lad of his years," Nial said. "He'll wake up in an hour with a headache, but otherwise he will be fine."

"Put him in a boat and tie him up," Nial commanded. "And now," raising his voice, "to Bannavem, where there are both rich booty and strong men for us to capture."

COMPREHENSION QUESTIONS

1. Why did Calpornius put on white robes?
2. About what did Calpornius warn his son?
3. Who was Julius?
4. Why did the Celtic warriors want to attack Bannavem?
5. How did Patricius get captured by King Nial?
6. Where did King Nial send Patrick after he captured him?

WORDS TO KNOW

booty	crevices
unconscious	embedded
bellowed	plunder
tragedy	ruthless

CHAPTER 4

Voyage to a New Land

Patricius did not wake up in an hour as Nial had said he would. It was several hours before Patricius began to return to consciousness. First, he became aware of a rolling motion, then he began to ask himself, "Where am I?" He soon realized that he was not in his comfortable bed in the farmhouse. The young captive tried to get up but found that he could barely move. A short time later, his memory came back and he became aware that his hands were tied behind his back. His legs were also tied. Patricius was lying on wooden planks, and he quickly realized that the rolling motion he had felt was caused by the swelling of the sea. He was now a captive of the Celts—a prisoner!

When the young lad opened his eyes, he saw the pale moon almost overhead. It was a clear night—the stars seemed very close, but Patricius knew that they were no closer than his father's house. Both seemed an eternity away, for he knew that the Irish raiders made slaves of their captives and put them to work. His future seemed dark as he thought about being a slave in a wild country until the day he died.

As Patricius choked back a tear, a Celtic warrior named Claith bent over him. He spoke in a kindly tone, but the boy didn't understand what he said. Then Claith untied him and rubbed his wrists to send the blood coursing through his veins. He held out a canteen made of goatskin, and Patricius eagerly swallowed the cool water it contained.

When Patricius was more comfortable, the Celtic warrior pointed to the sea and laughed while he said something in his own tongue. The young captive did not need a translator, for it was obvious what the man was saying. "Don't try to escape, lad. There is no place to go but to the bottom of the sea!"

As Patricius became accustomed to the semi-darkness, he looked around the ship. There were several men bound on either side of him, letting out occasional groans. Claith was going from man to man, slowly untying the miserable captives.

Patricius began to stand up near the center of the ship. He was relieved to find out that he had no broken bones. His head still hurt a great deal but his greatest concern was his broken heart. The young captive bitterly reflected upon the fact that he might never see his gentle mother or his caring father again.

As Patricius sat down in the ship once again, it was as if a tiny voice had flashed a message into his aching head. The message was a gentle reminder that he still had plenty for which to be thankful. "You are still alive and

well, Patricius," the voice seemed to say. As helpful as this message was to the lonely boy, it sparked a much more serious thought in his mind. "Why?" thought Patricius. "That fall from the cliff might very well have killed me; yet I am still alive. Could it be that my parents were right all along and God truly does have a plan for my life?"

As these thoughts began to slowly pass away, a strange peace began to come upon the young prisoner, as well as a profound sense of weariness. It was not long before the gentle rolling of the boat put Patricius into a deep sleep.

When he awoke, it was almost dawn. He sat up and watched the strong backs of the oarsmen bending forward and backward. The large boat slid smoothly through the water as Patricius heard someone nearby call "Patricius my young lad!" His heart jumped slightly as he quickly turned to see who it was that had called him. To his surprise, Patricius looked upon his old tutor and friend, Julius of Bannavem.

"I thought that I would never hear my native tongue spoken again," said Patricius. "Have you heard any news of my father and mother?"

Julius shook his head. "Very little, I'm afraid," he said sadly. "I was in the village at the council meeting when we heard the barking of dogs. Your father looked up and said quickly, 'Someone hurry and find out why the dogs are barking.' Centus, the blacksmith, ran from the room and climbed to the roof of the council hall. In a little while he came back crying. 'Raiders! Raiders! Foreign invaders are marching toward the east wall!'"

As Patricius sat and listened to his friend, he could imagine the despair that had gripped his father and the other members of the council. Bannavem, like most British villages in those days, was surrounded by a wall that the Roman soldiers had built nearly a century before. In the wall were two huge gates, one opening to the east and another to the west. The wooden gates were strong, and the brick-and-stone walls were sturdy. A handful of Roman soldiers could have defended the village against a force twice the size of Nial's, but there were no soldiers in Bannavem that day.

Julius broke in upon the young captives thoughts and continued his sad story. "Your father called out, 'Close the east gate and get all the women and children out of the west gate.' Everyone hurried to obey his orders."

"Did you close the gate in time?" Patricius asked.

Julius nodded. "Yes, and we told the women and children to leave the village through the west gate. The raiders, however, had come prepared with a huge battering ram. Fifty men held it and began to hammer away. As we waited behind the wall we could hear the big gate creaking and weakening. Then the gate fell with a mighty crash, and the raiders poured into Bannavem. We fought with the only weapons we had, rocks and sticks, but we were helpless against the Irish warriors."

"But what happened to my mother and father?" Patricius insisted. "Where are they?"

"I do not know," Julius responded. "I was so busy trying to defend the village that…well… I lost track of most everything in the confusion. The last time I looked upon your father, he was swinging a large club against the raiders. As for your mother, she was trying to put out a fire that had been started in a home nearby, before she disappeared from my sight. A short time later, I was hit on the head with the back of a sword, and when I recovered, I was sitting on a beach as a bound prisoner. A large number of captives were sitting nearby, most of them young men from other villages."

"Was my father among you?" Patricius asked. "Could he be in one of the other boats?"

Julius shook his head. "Neither he nor your mother were among us. They may have escaped through the west wall."

"They are probably dead," responded Patricius tearfully as he bowed his head in grief.

"Only the good Lord knows for sure," stated Julius. "It is easy to have faith in God when things are going well, but the real test comes when you have to accept God's will when things don't make sense. If you have faith in God, Patricius, you will be able to accept His will regarding your parents. Do the wise thing, my friend, and trust God in the same way that your father and mother have in the past."

Patricius said nothing, but gradually the painful throb of his sorrowful heart dulled. Julius was right as usual. And for all he knew, it was indeed possible that God had preserved his parents and that they were back on their farm safe and sound.

The big boat slipped easily through the calm sea. At regular periods the oarsmen were relieved by others. The boats stayed close to each other and the fleet moved on steadily through the early morning. Patricius noticed that one boat, larger than the rest, led the way. From its prow, there flew a red and blue banner, and Patricius correctly guessed that this was the king's boat. As difficult as it was, the young Briton had to admit that Nial was a skillful leader and knowledgeable sailor.

All that day the heavily laden vessels moved north toward that part of Ireland where Nial had his castle. On the morning of the third day at sea, Patricius was awakened by wild shouts. He looked ahead and soon saw land. The oarsmen rowed faster and smiles began to appear on their faces.

Patricius looked at them, and in that moment, he learned a lesson that some people never learn. This curious Briton came to realize that even savage people and fierce warriors can have a deep love for their lands and families. "Perhaps," young Patricius thought, "all men have the same basic needs and desires in their hearts." If this were true, perhaps captivity would not be as bad as he had expected it to be.

There was a great crowd waiting at the shore to meet their chieftain and his victorious raiders. As the men waded through the shallow water to shore, wives and children threw their arms around the necks of husbands and fathers.

Claith motioned for the prisoners to stop talking and to leave the boat. The captives were a miserable lot. Many wore bandages to cover their wounds and all of them were hungry and cold. They were herded through the crowd, which had come to the shore, as they struggled to keep warm in the cold morning air. Some of the people looked at the captives with pity, but most of them were merely curious. Patricius grew more and more discouraged as he looked at the faces of these strangers. As lonely as he was, he was finding it difficult to look forward to his sixteenth birthday. In spite of the encouragement of his friend Julius, Patricius saw little reason to hope that his situation would soon improve.

COMPREHENSION QUESTIONS

1. Who was the warrior who untied Patricius?
2. Who did Patricius meet while he was sailing?
3. Where did King Nial take Patricius and the other captives?
4. Did the warriors of King Nial capture the city of Bannavem?
5. How did the Irish warriors react when they saw their homeland?
6. What did Patricius admit about King Nial?

WORDS TO KNOW

translator	despair
accustomed	curious
profound	laden
native	captivity

CHAPTER 5

Patricius Becomes a Slave

The captives were marched for two miles until they came to King Nial's small castle. The stone build ing was like nothing Patricius had ever seen, for the Romans seldom built castles—they depended upon the walls around the towns to protect them. This was an amazing sight for a boy who had never before been more than ten miles away from Bannavem.

Beyond the castle, there were many long buildings and storage places for crops. There were pens, too, which kept the hogs and cattle from straying away. Patricius had managed to stay close to his friend Julius during the long march and soon turned to him for an explanation of what they saw.

"That is where we shall be working if we stay here," Julius said, pointing to the farm buildings.

"Of course we'll stay here. Where else would we go?" Patricius asked.

"I'll explain," Julius smiled. "There are over one hundred of us. Now, according to Irish custom, we are slaves of King Nial, but he has no use for a hundred slaves. So, many of us will be sold. All the chieftains who swear allegiance to him will be asked to come and look us over. They will bid for us. We will probably be sold to the highest bidders, who will pay Nial in gold, silver, or livestock."

"The boats that carried us to this strange land were also filled with stolen goods from our villages and farms," Patricius reminded Julius. "Does that all go to Nial too?"

"No, it will be divided among his men. That is how he attracts warriors to his cause. He promises them rich booty and," Julius added bitterly, "I'm afraid he kept his promise this time."

The young captive suddenly raised his head. "Listen!" he said. It's a bird singing."

"Yes, that is a blackbird," Julius said. "This is a country of song, my young friend. There are larks and nightingales and many birds which never come to our part of the world. Perhaps it is the music of the birds that has given these people such a great love of song. While they sing, they play strange, soft music on instruments similar to our harps and lutes."

"Shall we get a chance to hear them?" Patricius asked.

Julius nodded. "Unless I am mistaken, it is the custom of Irish kings to hold a great feast with plenty of food and music to celebrate a victory. Then, after we are well-fed and washed up to look our best, we will be sold at the close of the feast."

For three days the captives rested. Twice a day they were led out to eat simple but nourishing food. On more than one occasion, the prisoners were brought to a nearby river and told to bathe themselves and clean up their clothes.

"Nial wants us to look our best for the auction," Julius explained.

The next morning, Patricius noticed the preparations being made for the feast. Wild-looking chieftains began to arrive at the castle courtyard, and as they were recognized, loud greetings were called back and forth.

As soon as darkness fell, the chieftains, princes, and warriors marched into the great hall for the banquet. Nial sat at the head of the long table. He was dressed in purple, and a gold chain hung from his neck as a sign of his kingship. The food was served by the women, who brought in huge platters of steaming hot meat. The men picked up big chunks of ham and venison and devoured them with their strong teeth. They washed down the food with a special drink called "mead" that was made from boiled honeycombs.

At least a dozen of Nial's huge Irish wolfhounds were in the great hall. Guests threw them bones and bits of meat. And then for the first time, Patricius heard a song played on the harp. The rough, tough warriors quieted down as the bard (minstrel) ran his fingers over the strings of the harp and began to sing.

"He is a wandering bard," Julius explained. "He has composed a song about their great victory over our neighbors in Bannavem."

"A great victory, indeed!" Patricius exploded. "Why, our men had no swords or shields, they were defenseless. These heroes captured an unarmed village occupied by women and children."

"The bard wasn't there," Julius said plainly. "Anyhow,

it is his job to entertain the sea king and his warriors. A hundred years from now other musicians will be singing this song and people will believe that Nial won a wonderful military victory. These people do not write as the Romans do. The bards are their poets and their historians. People like to repeat the songs they compose."

When the bard had ended his song, the whole company applauded enthusiastically. They stamped on the floor and pounded the wooden tables in front of them. When they were quiet once more, Nial stood on his table and raised his hand for attention. Then he announced that the slaves were about to go on sale. "Bring them in!" shouted the Irish king. Within a few minutes, all of the captives, including Patricius and Julius, were herded into the huge banquet hall. Nial was quick to point out to the assembly that most of the prisoners for sale were skilled farmers, craftsmen, and experienced hunters.

One by one, the captives were brought forward. As Nial described each one, the chieftains called out their bids in loud, excited voices. As the captives were sold they were led outside to be guarded by representatives of the Celtic ruler who had bought them.

Finally, a warrior shoved Patricius forward. As he stood there, sturdy and proud before the great company, the light from the huge fire flickered on his boyish face. Nial began to talk. Julius, who was standing in back of the youth, whispered, "He is telling great lies about you. He is saying you are so brave that you fought until you were unconscious, and that finally it took six men to tie you up."

Patrick was tempted to smile after hearing the words of his friend. "The king's lies are most flattering," thought the young slave.

As soon as the king was finished talking, a dozen voices cried out offers for the strong lad. Then a man who had not bid with the others spoke up. Every eye looked upon this proud Irish chieftain as the room became strangely quiet.

Julius whispered, "I overheard the men call him Miliucc. He is supposed to be not only a mighty chieftain but also a Druid, as these pagans call the priests of their false religion. We would say that he practices the black arts, or that he is a sorcerer. Listen! He is offering six hogs and a silver chain for you. The others are afraid to bid against this man, lest he cast a spell on them."

A moment later, Nial cried out, "O holy Miliucc, the lad is your slave. You have made a wise choice, for this boy is a strong and useful farmhand." There was a great shout of approval from the assembled chieftains as Patricius was led out of the great hall.

As the slaves were preparing to sleep for the last time in Nial's castle, Julius came over to Patricius to say his farewell.

"I was told that in the morning you will be taken north to a small town called Antrim nestled in the Slemish Mountains. It is a five-day march," added Julius, quietly.

The discouraged young lad was trying in vain to fight back tears as he grasped Julius' firmly. "I will miss your wise counsel and caring spirit my dear friend," whispered Patricius.

"This parting is indeed a sad one, but I pray that the Lord would cause even this event to work together for your good," said Julius with a firm resolve.

"Now we had best get to sleep lad," added Julius, "for we will both need our strength for the journey tomorrow. I am bound for a farm several miles to the south."

As Patricius prepared for bed and an uncertain future, he looked up at the stars of heaven. "How can I survive in this world of chaos all by myself?" thought the young slave. "O how I wish I had the simple faith and hope of men like Julius and my father."

In the providence of God, the lonely and confused sinner named Patricius would not have long to wait for his spiritual desires to be blessed by his Maker.

COMPREHENSION QUESTIONS

1. How many captives were brought to Ireland by King Nial?
2. Did the Romans like to build castles?
3. Who sang at the slave auction?
4. What role did the Irish bards play in their society?
5. Who bought Patricius at the slave auction?
6. Where was Julius sent after he was sold?

WORDS TO KNOW

parting	bard
resolve	nourishing
military	allegiance
bidder	livestock

CHAPTER 6

Life Among the Druids

The march north was a tiring one. Miliucc and a
dozen of the Druids' most important men rode in
chariots drawn by horses, but his soldiers and captives were forced to walk. On several occasions, Patricius
was hard pressed to keep pace with the chariots. His strong
and youthful body, however, managed to help him en-
dure the hardship of the five-day journey to the Slemish
Mountains.

Patricius struggled to learn the simple commands that
were given to him along the way. His old friend Julius
had attempted to tutor him in the Irish language known
as Gaelic so he could understand his captors. Regretta-
bly, however, the young slave from Bannavem did not
have enough time to learn a great deal of Gaelic before
he was separated from his gifted tutor and friend.
Patricius, therefore, would be required to pick up the
strange new language of his captors as best as he could
over a long period of time.

As the caravan of chariots and men approached the
small castle where Miliucc lived, Patricius could think of
little else but food. He, like most of the men, was extremely
hungry, cold, and tired. The chief steward of the castle
came out to greet the assembly and quickly ordered the

guards to transport the new slaves to a set of thatched roof buildings located nearby. Within minutes, the guards had deposited the slaves in their new quarters and introduced these hungry men to the castle dogs. It was plainly evident that the dogs were trained to hunt men and would, therefore, pose a serious problem to any one who was thinking about trying to escape. With simple but effective sign language, the guards also made it very clear that the penalty for trying to escape was death.

Each of the hungry men was given a water pouch made from goatskin, a piece of hard black bread, and a sheepskin blanket to sleep on. These simple provisions seemed like luxuries to the desperate men who were so far from home.

Meanwhile, Miliucc's people came running out to greet their chief. At the head of this assembly were his three children and his favorite dog. As is often the case the world over, Miliucc's children wanted to know if he had brought them presents. "I have no presents, children, except a new group of slaves for you to play with," said the impatient father in his Gaelic tongue.

One of Miliucc's sons, named Einar, asked if any of the new slaves were close to his age. "I think there is at least one boy who is close to your age," replied Miliucc. "You will have to ask the guards to take you down to the slave quarters on the morrow," added the weary chief as he walked slowly to his grey stone castle.

The next morning, the teenager named Einar made his way over to the thatched huts were Patricius lived. One of the guards told Patricius to spend time with Einar, but the young slave could barely understand what he was telling him. After a few minutes of trying to talk with Miliucc's

son, Patricius decided to ask Einar to teach him the Gaelic
language.

When Einar finally understood that the young slave
wanted to learn Gaelic, he began to smile and nod his head.
Each boy made a game of teaching the other his language.
Einar did not progress very far in learning Latin, but
Patricius began to learn Gaelic quickly.

It was often difficult for Patricius
to find time to play and learn with his
new companion, for he was sent
to the fields almost every
day to sharpen his
s h e p h e r d i n g
skills. In spite of
these   circum-
stances, the young
shepherd slave was
able to go fishing
and swimming in a

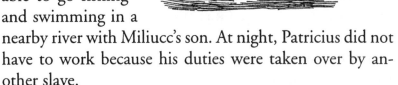

nearby river with Miliucc's son. At night, Patricius did not
have to work because his duties were taken over by another slave.

As the weeks flew by, Patricius spent more time tending the sheep and hogs which grazed on the hillsides and
in the valley. The young British slave treasured every hour
that he could spend with his new friend, for the life of a
shepherd was lonely in the extreme.

In the evening hours, Patricius would walk back to
his humble cottage and spend time talking with Einar.
Miliucc's son made a point of speaking to the shepherd
slave in Gaelic. He also attempted to teach Patricius about
the Druid traditions and religious practices. Einar, how-

ever, was unable to interest Patricius in the pagan religious rites of the Druids because Patricius was not interested in anything religious.

As autumn began to bring in cooler weather, Einar told his companion about an upcoming harvest festival that was sponsored by his father. The highlight of this annual pagan festival was a special sacrifice that was designed to appease the so-called "harvest gods." Every household in the area that followed the Druid priests and worshiped the "gods" of nature would be in attendance at the harvest festival.

Patricius thought very little of this event for he was more interested in minding his own business and staying out of trouble. After all, he had a rather comfortable life considering the fact that he was a slave. A few days later, Patricius did manage, however, to get up the courage to ask Einar if he had ever heard of the Christian religion. "Do the people of Ireland know anything about the religion of Christianity?" asked the curious slave from Britain.

Einar nodded. "We have people who worship a man called Christ in our country. But they have no leaders. For hundreds of years, Irish chieftains have been raiding Britain, always bringing back slaves. Hundreds of these slaves were followers of the Christian way and many of them refused to give up their religion. When they told others about this Jesus, some people believed their stories. But they fear the power of the Druids and the chieftains who rule our land."

"I did not know," Patricius said in a somewhat surprised voice.

"Why do you ask me these strange questions?" asked

Miliucc's son. "You are not one of those fools who worships the dead man called Christ, are you?" continued Einar.

"Why no, I don't think so—I mean no I don't care one way or the other about any religion," blurted out the embarrassed Patricius. "Let's talk about something else, shall we?"

"Very well," said Miliucc's son gruffly.

They were silent for several moments, and then Einar said "Get some sleep, Patricius. The night is upon us and you will undoubtedly be ordered to serve tables at the harvest festival tomorrow. If you know what is good for you, then you will do nothing to dishonor any of the Druid priests as they do their holy sacrifices."

As Einar began to trot back towards the castle, Patricius could not help but wonder what he was talking about. "Why would a slave like me care about the religious sacrifices of Druid priests?" he thought. As these questions began to press upon the young shepherd slave, he quickly decided that it was silly to worry about something that he had no ability to understand. Moments later, Patricius made his way over to his sheepskin blanket and fell fast asleep.

The next morning, as predicted, Patricius found himself under the direction of the castle steward who was making final preparations for the daylong harvest festival. Miliucc, the high priest, was moving about the castle on a regular basis barking out commands. He was dressed in his official white priestly robes.

By mid-morning, several hundred families were moving about the castle grounds as the sun began to warm the cold air. After a while, shouts of laughter could be heard in various parts of the castle as the people witnessed magic shows and mock sword fights. The sounds of harps and minstrels singing also filled the air, as the crowd enjoyed good food and amusing games.

As the afternoon drew on, Patricius was more puzzled than ever about Einar's remarks from the previous night. Thus far the harvest festival had been quite tame and anything but strange. Moments later, however, Miliucc stood up in the midst of the crowd and raised his hands. As he prepared to speak, a hush suddenly came upon the assembly.

Miliucc addressed the people by saying, "In the holy name of the Lord of harvest, I command every soul to prepare itself for the sacrifice. Our faithful harvest gods must be appeased or they will take vengeance upon our crops and animals! Bring, therefore, the young child forward and pile the stones near the sacrifice."

Patricius watched in horror and disbelief as Miliucc commanded a number of men and women to murder a tiny girl in cold blood. As the stones knocked the life out of the poor girl, Patricius cried out "Stop, stop hurting the girl!"

No sooner had the words left the mouth of the terrified slave than a group of warriors began to grab a hold of him. Seconds later, the high priest ordered these men to remove Patricius to the castle dungeon where they were to punish him for his "unholy acts."

The frightened slave spent a miserable night in the dark prison cell after receiving many harsh beatings throughout the evening hours. Around midnight, Miliucc himself paid a visit to the young slave and told him that he would no longer enjoy the easy life. "You will be banished from my estate on the morrow. I hope you die a miserable and slow death as you tend my sheep and pigs in the wilderness country. May the cursing of the harvest gods be upon you!"

By this time, Patricius was so sore and tired that he barely heard the ramblings of the Druid high priest. Shortly after the angry priest left the dungeon, Patricius began to feel an emptiness within his soul. Part of him simply hated the evil and foolish traditions of the Druids. Nevertheless, a greater part of his soul was terrified as he came to the realization that he was, in his own way, just as wicked as Miliucc.

Tears began to flow once again down the prisoner's face. This time, however, the tears were not just because he was sad or lonely, Patricius was grieving because he finally saw how his own sins were an offense to God. In the midst of his despair, Patricius was comforted somewhat by the message that his father had given him as a boy. His father said, "Trust in God my son, and do not lean upon your own understanding, in all thy ways acknowledge Him and He shall direct your paths."

Before the weary slave fell into a deep sleep, he tried to utter a simple but earnest prayer. "Dear God, I need a Savior. Help me to trust in Christ and direct my paths out of this foul dungeon."

COMPREHENSION QUESTIONS

1. What language did the people in Ireland speak?
2. What was the name of Miliucc's son?
3. Who did the Christians in Ireland fear?
4. What did Patricius do when he saw the girl stoned?
5. Who visited Patricius when he was in the dungeon?
6. What did Patricius realize after he was in the dungeon?

WORDS TO KNOW

luxuries	weary
appeased	captors
dungeon	deposited
quarters	provisions

CHAPTER 7

A Shepherd Named Patrick

In answer to his prayer, Patricius was taken from his dark dungeon cell and placed in a cart that was heading for a distant location. He had no idea where the guards were taking him, but wherever it was it could not be more depressing than a dungeon, he thought. As the cart bumped along the road, the shepherd slave could barely keep from shivering in the winter air.

The winter did not creep up gently on Ireland that year. It burst upon the land savagely, with great storms. The little creatures of the forest crept into hollow tree trunks, burrowed into the ground, or fled to the hills in search of small caves. The wolves, which had been well-fed all summer, became hungry and vicious. Their natural prey was gone, so they went looking for sheep and hogs and cows.

Patricius was no longer allowed to go back to a warm barn at night. He and the shepherds he helped had to remain with the flocks all night, for it was then that the wolves came. It was lonely on top of the hill called Skerry, and the wind blowing in from the sea bit through his thin clothes. Sometimes, when Patricius was in the field at night, he would doze off. Often, however, the howl of a wolf would rudely wake him up, then he would throw wood upon the fires, which were never allowed to die, and proceed to walk among the frightened sheep with soothing words.

When the icy rains came and blasts of snow blew in from the sea, the young slave from Bannavem wondered whether he could live through the winter. Yet, it was more than physical discomfort that troubled him. It was lonely in the hills, and Patricius, to comfort his loneliness, prayed. He found that when he prayed he was no longer lonely. Even though he had prayed many times in the past, this time it was different. He truly felt the presence and abiding comfort of God as he poured out his heart in Jesus' name.

Once again, Patricius thought of the words of his beloved father who had once said, "My son, if you have God in your heart you are never alone." And Patricius found that in this area, as in all other things, his father spoke the truth.

One morning before light, the spiritually alive teenager rose up to pray. He prayed without ceasing as the hours of the morning moved on, as if in search for something. Finally, the lonely sinner named Patricius began to sense the love and fear of God surrounding him. Faith to believe the words of Scripture arose in his heart, and with this faith a greater understanding of his sin. Patricius repented of his sin and committed his helpless soul to God, asking that Jesus Christ would be his Lord and Savior. From that point on, Patricius began a wonderful spiritual pilgrimage with the triune God of Scripture as his Guide. The frightened boy, Patricius, had been called in the providence of Almighty God to grow up into the true and courageous servant of Christ we now know as Saint Patrick.

The daily routine of Patrick was designed to permit him to survive the lonely and harsh conditions of a shepherd in the cold wilderness. Every morning, Patrick would get up before daylight to pray, whether in snow or frost or rain. In a single day, this shepherd boy would pray as often as a hundred times, as the Spirit of God was working in a mighty way to strengthen his faith. No matter how hungry or cold Patrick became, the Lord enabled him to stay healthy and joyful.

One night, five of the sheep were carried off by wolves. It was not Patrick's fault, nor was it the fault of the other

shepherds. The wolves were so desperate with hunger that they no longer feared the roaring fires. They came not in pairs—they came in large packs often numbering twenty beasts. Then, while Patrick and the shepherds were driving the wolves away from one side of the hill, a few would slip in from the other side and drag away the defenseless lambs. After several nights of this madness, the head shepherd finally decided that the sheep should be brought back to the barnyards every night.

At dusk each day, therefore, it was Patrick's job to bring a flock back from the hills to the barns, where they would be safe. It was a long three-mile journey, but Patrick did not mind; he rather enjoyed the chance to meet a few of the servants that were living near the barns.

Patrick would now be able to regularly meet with the cook and serving women who were responsible for giving the shepherds a daily portion of meat or soup. These servants grew to know and like Patrick. He would sit almost unnoticed and listen to them talk about the issues of every day life. Sometimes these simple Irish peasants would tell stories about ancient Irish kings like Ossian and Finn MacCool. The latter was, they said, the strongest man who ever lived. On some occasions, a distant howling would disturb the peace of the night, and the old women would mutter about souls in torment and explain that the souls of evil people came back in the forms of animals.

"If a little child dies, does he return?" Patrick would ask, eager to know all he could about the beliefs of the Irish.

"Of course, lad," he would be told. "They came back as lovely butterflies."

"Don't you believe in Heaven?" he would ask.

"Heaven? What is that?" they would ask, puzzled.

Patrick would turn away, and then spend long hours pondering how best to answer the question.

In many respects, the shepherd boy Patrick was not unlike the shepherd from ancient Israel named David. Both of these young men were saved in their youth, and yet they were driven into the wilderness to be refined and purified through many trials. Neither David nor Patrick would have become tender and courageous leaders in manhood if God had not brought them through many difficult trials and testings in their youth.

COMPREHENSION QUESTIONS

1. Where was Patricius taken after he was released from the dungeon?
2. What type of work did Patricius do for Miliucc?
3. What did Patrick do to help cope with his cold and lonely circumstances?
4. Did Patrick ever come to faith in Christ?
5. What did the common people in Ireland know about heaven?
6. In what way was Patrick like the shepherd boy David of Israel?

WORDS TO KNOW

refined	mutter
purified	peasant
torment	pilgrimage
triune	providence

CHAPTER 8

Life Among the Irish

The winter passed, summer came, and then there was another winter. Still another year came and went, and now Patrick had reached his full size. At nineteen, he was tall and broad-shouldered.

During the years that Patrick had spent as a shepherd-slave, he had learned to live with the cold winters. The open fields were his home much of the time. He had no fear at all of the wolves or the wild boars or any of the savage beasts that tried so hard to get to the livestock. Over the years, Patrick had also been able to develop a small but joyful band of friends who worked on nearby farms.

At this time in Patrick's life, he had come to understand the people of Ireland. They were wild and savage, he felt, because they were restless sinners. The pagan Irish usually lacked the faith to comfort themselves in bad times or in sorrow, and had nothing to look forward to after death. Many Irish people believed that they would return in the form of animals after their life was over. Others believed that death ended everything. None of them, except the few Christians that were in the land believed in a glorious life after death.

One afternoon, Patrick asked his friend Alfred, who was a local shepherd, whether any Christian missionaries were active in Ireland. "There are many Christian preachers who have tried to give out the message," Alfred began. "They go around the countryside preaching your faith, but eventually the kings and Druids find them and kill them. I have heard many reports, but usually the people mock the ones who try to bring them any religious message anyway," said the elderly shepherd.

"If God sent a man to convert these people, they would not be able to resist the power of the gospel forever," Patrick said.

"Perhaps you are right, someday my people may change their minds regarding your God. But don't set your hopes too high, my friend," added Alfred with a smile.

On another occasion, some weeks later, Alfred noticed once again that Patrick had eaten only half of his rations. The old shepherd had often asked his young friend about this, but Patrick had never given him an explanation. Alfred often asked him why he half-starved himself, and finally one day, Patrick told him.

"You know I am a Christian," he said. "And I worship the Lord Jesus Christ. There are many ways for me to show love for my Master. One way is by fasting. It reminds me of how He fasted and how He suffered and died for me."

"For you, maybe," said the faithless shepherd. "But

not for me. Why should I need a Savior anyway?"

"You need a Savior, Alfred, for the simple reason that you are a sinner. And it is your sinfulness that keeps you separated from the love and righteousness of the Creator God Jesus Christ."

"Tell me about Him," begged the curious seeker.

So Patrick told his friend the whole story of Jesus as he remembered it from his childhood. He told him how Jesus was born in a manger, how he was unjustly killed by being nailed to a cross, how He arose after His death, and then how, forty days later, He ascended into Heaven. Alfred listened attentively as Patrick also explained, the triune nature of the Godhead as Father, Son, and Holy Spirit.

"The Father of Jesus was the most powerful of all gods. Is that it?" Alfred asked.

"He was and is the only true God," Patrick corrected him.

"Well, then," the old shepherd continued, "when they nailed Jesus to the cross, why didn't He call to His Father for help?"

"Because Jesus loved His chosen people so much that He was willing to offer up His life as a sacrifice to pay for the sins of those people," Patrick said. "Let me try to explain. You have many harsh laws that are binding under the pain of death. If a man steals from his neighbor, for example, he is punished for his offense by death. Even if a very poor man steals, he breaks the law, and no matter what the excuse, he must die. Am I right?"

Alfred nodded his head. "Of course."

"Nobody can save his life—unless the king pardons him. Is not that the law of the land?" Patrick continued.

The curious shepherd looked puzzled. "Of course,"

he replied impatiently. "This is well known to all. It is the law handed down by our fathers."

"But then," and Patrick looked straight at Alfred, "suppose your mightiest king spoke out and said, 'This man is under my protection. He is a member of my royal family. I command that the judge pardon him as a member of my household, and I will pay back anything he has stolen and make things right....' What would happen then?" asked Patrick.

There was a moment of silence. Then Alfred, swelling his chest, replied in a loud voice, "The king would make sure that his family member was set free and would pay the person's debt honorably."

"Well," said Patrick, "in a way, something like that happens when guilty sinners like us come before the Judge of all the earth. To pay the penalty for our sin, which is everlasting death, the Almighty King graciously offers His own Son to suffer and die in order to pay our sin debt. Like your poor man who stole, we human beings are helpless to pay for our sins for we are dead in our trespasses and guilt. God must, therefore, provide the payment.

"The Good News, Alfred, is that God has provided a Savior for His people. Jesus Christ, who is God as well as man came into the world and died on the cross to cancel the sin debt for everyone who believes. It is Jesus who is the great sin-bearer. It is He who died in our place. Now He speaks to God the Father on behalf of those for whom He died and says—pardon them."

Patrick closed his message by telling Alfred that, "In a manner similar to your noble kings, God has accepted the sacrifice of Christ as full payment for our sins. He is willing to forgive us—and to give us a new life. We must, however, repent of our sins and trust in the righteousness of His Son, Jesus Christ."

"I find some of this hard to understand," Alfred said.

"It does require some serious thought," Patrick admitted. "Above all, however, it requires a humble and willing mind to understand the truth of God's salvation. No individual can comprehend or accept the gospel of Christ without the help of God. Hopefully, someday, if God wills, you will be able to believe the gospel message. If you are given the gift of faith in God, you will never need to fear—not even death, because you will know that there is a better life waiting for you in Heaven than you could possibly have on earth.

"If the Druid priests heard you talking about the Christian way, they would toss you back in one of their dark dungeons. How do you know that I will not report you to our priests?" questioned Alfred.

"I cannot be certain what you will do with the truths I have told you. All I know is that I have the duty to share the gospel of Christ," said Patrick sincerely. "Because I know that the Lord God is my Savior and Protector, I do not need to fear prison or even death."

"Everyone I know, including my Druid priest, fears death," Alfred responded with awe. "It must be wonderful to worship a God who promises you a life after death and gives you such strength to serve Him each day."

"It is," Patrick agreed. "But each soul must make peace with God through Christ for himself. The gift of eternal life is only open to those who are humble enough to repent and trust in the death and resurrection of Christ."

"I wish I could remember everything you have told me today," said the old shepherd. "Will you tell the story of Jesus to my sisters?"

"Of course," Patrick assured him.

Two weeks later, Alfred's sisters stopped by to talk with Patrick while he was feeding some hogs. Both women asked many questions and listened attentively as Patrick told them the things in which he believed. He was so sincere and earnest in stating the truths of the message of Christ that his words made a deep impression on the women.

"Our older brother and the rest of our family worships the god of the sun and moon. We also have a god of the sea and a god of the wind. Are you saying that these gods are false?" asked the women.

"Yes. You have heard me correctly," said Patrick softly. "The one true God is Lord over all of His creation. He controls everything in the world, including the sun, moon, wind, and sea."

"You must love your God very much to speak so boldly," said each of the women.

"I do," Patrick said simply. "But even more important is the fact that I know He loves me. His perfect Son died to take away my sins. No mere man could love me that much."

"I can see why you follow this Christian God," they responded. "We worship our gods simply because we fear them and want to protect our families from their curses. I have never heard of any of our gods dying for us."

The winters came and went, the seasons passed into years, and still Patrick tended the sheep and the swine on the hills that rose above the valley. He was gripped now by a strange restlessness which he was unable to shake off. He prayed that God would grant him a contented spirit, but the Lord would not give him a sense of peace.

"I must escape from here, Alfred," he said one day after he had spent almost six years as a shepherd slave. "I am wasting my life tending sheep and swine. I have had many dreams lately, and they disturb me. In them, I hear a voice which tells me that Jesus is pleased because I fast and pray and keep His commandments. And then the voice says, 'Wait, Patrick, wait.'

"What shall I do, Alfred?" begged the troubled slave.

"It sounds like you have little choice but to do what you are told," Alfred advised. "Wait, lad, just wait."

COMPREHENSION QUESTIONS

1. What did Patrick understand about the Irish people?
2. Who was Alfred?
3. What does it mean to fast?
4. Why didn't Jesus call out to His Father for help as He hung on the cross?
5. Why can't human beings pay for their own sins?
6. Why don't Christians need to fear death?

WORDS TO KNOW

impression	pardon
convert	debt
explanation	righteousness
trespasses	protector

CHAPTER 9

The Long Road Home

Patrick was now a grown man of twenty-one years of age. He had spent six years in the service of the Druid leader, Miliucc. Although he had come to know the language and customs of Ireland, he still felt he belonged to the land of his birth. Patrick had often spent many sleepless nights wondering if his parents were still alive. He prayed for them constantly.

One night, unable to sleep, he walked to the top of Skerry Hill. He often went there to pray. The moonlight streamed down upon the countryside and the cool night air felt good on his brow. From the hill he could see the flock sleeping contentedly, because it was summer now, the wolves were deep in the forest.

Kneeling in the soft moonlight, he asked God to forgive him his sins. He asked if there were any way in which he could serve the God he loved and begged for guidance. All during the night he prayed, until the first shafts of the sun began to appear on the horizon. Patrick looked toward the sun and marveled at the miracle that God performed every morning.

As night turned into day, Patrick began to doze off for a few minutes. Suddenly, he seemed to hear a voice which spoke to him saying, "Fast well, for soon you will be going back to your own country." When Patrick finally opened his eyes again, the countryside looked no different than on other mornings. The sun was filling the valley below and the birds were singing merrily. Try as he might, the confused shepherd tried to figure out where the voice had come from, but to no avail.

Later that day, after lunch time, Patrick decided to take a short nap. Once again, a voice spoke to him saying, "See, your ship is ready."

Patrick soon arose trembling with joy. He believed that an angel of the Lord was at long last directing him to escape. He was confident that he knew what he had to do, even though his Druid master would be furious when he found out that he had escaped.

"I shall leave tonight after dark," thought the confident slave. "If the Lord has a ship ready for me, I must trust Him to guide my steps in the right direction."

As Patrick revealed his plans to his trusted friend, Alfred, he began to get very anxious in his spirit. Alfred was quick to point out the dangers involved in such a journey, as he warned Patrick to watch out for the guard dogs. "The big wolfhounds are trained to bark loudly when any slave tries to escape," asserted the old shepherd.

"Thank you for your concern old friend," said Patrick. "I have spent almost six years with these guard dogs, Alfred. They should not give me any problems."

As the moon began to appear in the night sky, Patrick gave a farewell hug to his old friend, Alfred. Even as the escaping slave moved tearfully down the muddy lane, some of the wolfhounds came forward and licked his hand, as though to bid him a fond farewell. It was an encouragement for Patrick to know that he would not be troubled by the guard dogs.

The escaping slave walked all night in a southeasterly direction, stopping for brief periods at farmhouses along the way to obtain food. Patrick traveled on in his walk of faith for several days, hoping to get to a seacoast town that had a port. After traveling over one hundred miles through the Irish countryside, Patrick finally found himself on a hill overlooking the Irish Sea.

"And there," said Patrick calmly as he looked upon a large ship riding at anchor, "is the vessel that God has prepared for my deliverance."

Close to the shore was the largest ship that Patrick had ever seen. It was not like the fishing boats he had known as a child, nor was it like Nial's raiding vessels. It was larger than these ships, having two masts with large sails instead of oars.

Without a word, the optimistic slave walked down the hillside toward the harbor. He had nearly reached it when he encountered a farmer who greeted him in a friendly fashion.

"I am destined to sail on the ship that is in your harbor," Patrick told the stranger.

"It is waiting for the tide and will probably sail late this afternoon," said the farmer. "Why don't you come to my cottage and have something to eat before you visit the ship?" added the friendly stranger. "You look tired and hungry."

Tired and hungry was an accurate description of Patrick at this time, so he gladly accepted the farmer's invitation. As both men sat together they talked of many things and enjoyed a steaming hot bowl of mutton soup and fresh bread.

Patrick asked the stranger, "What news have you regarding King Nial of the Nine Hostages?"

"Nial is dead," the farmer said sadly. "All his life he lived by the sword and finally he died by the sword. He raided the land to the east called Britain one too many times, looking for slaves. The people of Britain finally became strong enough to fight Nial's men, and now he is dead. His young son Loegaire the Violent, rules in his place."

"May God have mercy on Nial's soul," Patrick said softly.

The farmer looked startled. "Are you a Christian then?" he asked very eagerly.

Patrick nodded, and the farmer said, "In these parts, there are many of us like you. We are merely waiting for the man who is to come one day and humble the proud kings so that God's lambs may breath free. That is the prophecy that many Druid priests have made as well."

"I will pray for the Lord to raise up just the right man for this noble task, my friend," said Patrick.

After the escaping slave had refreshed himself, he gave his warmest thanks to the gracious farmer and walked down to the sea. The ship was anchored about a hundred yards off shore. As Patrick stood admiring its rustic beauty, a rowboat came quietly dancing toward the shore. The men who landed made their way to a nearby spring and began to fill their kegs with fresh water. As they worked in the afternoon sun, Patrick decided to ask these men if they were from the big ship. Before he could speak, however, a huge bearded man looked curiously at Patrick and said, "Who are you?"

"My name is Patrick," was the response, "and I would like to take passage with you on your boat. I will work hard for my passage."

"Nonsense," the big man said. "I am the captain of the ship, and I have a full crew. We are leaving as soon as we replenish our water supply."

Patrick's heart sank.

Within a few moments the sailors returned. They placed the water-filled kegs in the boat and took their places at the oars. Soon the boat was once more headed toward the ship.

Patrick raised his eyes to heaven. "If this is indeed my boat," he prayed "I beg You to soften the heart of the captain. Make him return for me."

As he slowly began to walk away from the harbor area, he heard a voice in the distance. Patrick turned around, and a stranger yelled at him, "Do you know anything about wolfhounds?"

"I have been a shepherd for six years and I am very familiar with all kinds of dogs. I know how to handle and quiet wolfhounds if that is your need."

"In that case," said the sailor, "the captain gives you liberty to come along with us. Part of our cargo consists of twenty of these fierce beasts, and we need a man like you."

Patrick's eyes shone brightly—another answer to prayer. He ran quickly to the rowboat and stepped into the middle of the vessel. Now Patrick knew that his days of slavery were behind him by the grace of Almighty God.

COMPREHENSION QUESTIONS

1. How old was Patrick when he escaped from Irish slavery?
2. How did Patrick leave Ireland?
3. What prophecy did many Druid priests have?
4. How did King Nial die?
5. Who took care of Patrick shortly before he left Ireland?
6. Why did the captain finally decide to take Patrick on board?

WORDS TO KNOW

kegs	replenish
cargo	optimistic
mutton	encountered
prophecy	anxious

CHAPTER 10

Patrick's First Converts

An hour later, the tide changed and a fresh breeze sprang up. The captain gave quick, sharp commands, and the gleaming white sails were hoisted. The anchor was pulled up and the ship, as though glad to be away from the land, seemed to leap forward eagerly. It soon began to slip smoothly through the dark blue water.

Now the wolfhounds, tied together with heavy thongs, began to bark with excitement. The sailors edged away from them.

"These beasts are mad," a sailor muttered to Patrick.

"They are not mad," Patrick said with a smile, "only afraid. They have never felt the motion of a ship before."

Patrick walked across the deck to the dogs and spoke to them, using the familiar Gaelic words which they understood. They seemed to recognize the authority and the friendship in Patrick's voice, and their angry barks soon died down.

"You had best tell the captain that these animals need food and water soon," asserted Patrick to a nearby sailor. A few minutes later, two sailors returned carrying meat, water, and bones for the hungry dogs. It did not take long for these animals to devour the food and lap up the water.

Much to the captain's surprise, the previously unruly

dogs were now stretched out calmly on the deck, happily playing with the bones. Patrick sat down with the huge beasts and began to stroke several of their heads. The captain watched in amazement. He had thought of these dogs as being vicious, much like wolves, and yet this youth was sitting among them unafraid. He walked over and talked to Patrick.

"You spoke truly when you said that you can handle wolfhounds," he began.

"They are not really vicious, Captain," Patrick smiled. "They are seldom wild unless others make them so. By the way, Captain, how long will it take us to get to Britain?"

"Britain?" the Captain laughed. "We are not bound for Britain. We are going to Gaul and will land at a port named Burdigola (now known as Bordeaux, France). After our cargo is unloaded, we will be delivering some of the supplies to towns inland."

"But Gaul is not my destination," said the puzzled passenger.

"As to what your destination is, I do not care," the captain said bluntly. "My orders are to go to Gaul." He walked away, and Patrick stood there stunned and sick with disappointment.

The thought had simply never occurred to Patrick that the ship he felt led to board might not be going exactly where he wanted! As the wind picked up and the waves swelled slightly, the disturbed passenger and former slave thought to himself, "It does not pay to second guess God's ways. I must trust, as a child, the providence of God."

The ship headed south through the Irish Sea toward Gaul, which we now know as France. During the second night at sea, Patrick still found it hard to sleep on the hard wooden deck. For this reason, Patrick decided to use this time of sleeplessness for prayer. In the lonely Slemish Mountains, the former slave had always prayed aloud because there was no one to hear him but the animals, and now once again, without realizing it, he prayed aloud.

The captain, whose name was Noel, happened to be passing near Patrick and heard him praying. "To what god do you pray, young man?" the captain asked curiously.

"To the God of the Christians," Patrick said, "Who is the only true God."

"I have heard of this God in Gaul and also in Britain," the captain said. "I do not believe in Him myself. I believe in the gods of the wind and the sea, for these are the gods that bring us safely to port. However, young man," he said cheerfully, "pray to whatever god you wish. We shall need the help of all the gods to deliver our cargo safely."

Three days later, the ship arrived at the port of Burdigola. Everyone on board had expected to see a busy port and thriving city, instead they saw nothing but ruins and devastation. The northern European tribe, called the Vandals, had but recently raided Burdigola. After looting the homes and making slaves of the people, they had burned the city.

"I had expected to find food for us here," the captain asserted, "but the savages have taken everything. I shall leave six men to guard the ship, and the rest of us will immediately set off inland to find food and deliver our cargo. After we deliver our cargo and the dogs to the estate of Monsieur Gasston, we will be rich. But the journey across land will be long and hard."

The captain was right. On the fifth day, they found themselves in a trackless barren land—and with no food or water. They unloosed the dogs, hoping they could track down game. Two hours later, however, the animals returned, weary with their tongues hanging out. They had found nothing but a couple of rats.

That night, Patrick and the whole band of sailors dropped down on the ground and fell into a sleep of exhaustion. At dawn, Patrick awoke to pray as was his custom. He found the strength to continue after he spent time with God. As the morning unfolded, Captain Noel led his tired men south into the countryside. Day after day, week after week, they trudged through the desolate wasteland. On the twenty-eighth day, the captain came to Patrick for help.

"Half of my men are dead," he said hoarsely. "Unless we find food and water, the rest of us will soon die. I have prayed to my gods of the sea and the wind, and they have not answered me. You once told me on board my ship that your God was the one true God. Why do you not ask Him to save us? Can't you see that we are starving to death?"

Patrick stood up slowly and plainly told the entire group of men to forsake their false gods. "Turn in faith and with all your hearts to the Lord my God, for whom nothing is impossible," said Patrick loudly. "He will send you food until you have all you can eat, for he has abundance of it everywhere."

There in the barren wasteland, Patrick proceeded to kneel down and quietly pray. The sailors looked at him curiously but they did not laugh. They were starving and death was near, and they knew that their own gods had failed to answer their pleas. Could it be, they asked themselves, that there was another God who might save them?

As Patrick prayed, a cool breeze sprang up carrying

with it what seemed like the sound of hoof beats. The weary sailors grabbed their spears and their short swords. The sound of animals running became louder and louder, and then a herd of swine swept into view and headed directly for the little band of starving men. Summoning all of their strength, the sailors bore down upon the swine and slaughtered them.

A few of the sailors marched in the direction from which the swine had come, and to their great surprise found some old rotting logs, the first pieces of wood they had seen in twenty-eight days. They lit huge fires and cooked the meat. In one of the tree stumps they also found honey, which partly quenched their thirst. Only when they had eaten their fill did they remember that it was after Patrick had prayed that their needs were met.

"Tell us more about your God," Captain Noel said. "It was He who sent us this food and who directed us to the honey."

"If you would only have faith in Him," Patrick pleaded, "you would not want for food or any good gift."

The men remained quiet while he told them the story of Jesus and how He came to call lost sinners to repentance and faith. It was hard for them to accept it, for all their lives, they had worshipped such different gods. They listened, however, and did not scoff as Patrick told them how Christ had brought back the dead to life and how He had healed the lame and blind. Many of his listeners, at that moment, repented of their sins and accepted the God about whom Patrick spoke. These were his first converts.

The next morning, Captain Noel and his men continued the trip south. Later that afternoon, they reached a fertile area where fruit blossomed and game abounded. There was food for all, and cool springs provided plenty of fresh water. After refreshing themselves, the caravan of men resumed their journey and soon reached their destination.

Captain Noel was glad to deposit his cargo and wolfhounds at the estate of the rich landowner that was expecting him. After the business dealings were completed, Noel's men prepared to head back to Burdigola and their ship.

"Where is your ship bound for now captain?" asked Patrick.

"I suspect Spain or Italy will be next," said Noel plainly. "Why do you ask, are you thinking of leaving us Christian?"

"The thought had crossed my mind, Captain," confessed Patrick.

"Well, you had best make up your mind quickly," snapped the captain. "We start back to the ship tomorrow afternoon."

As he said this, they saw a group of travelers approaching. There were ten men wearing the long robes of monks.

"I wonder," Patrick thought to himself, "if these men are my new guides."

COMPREHENSION QUESTIONS

1. What job did Patrick perform while on board the ship?
2. What was the name of the captain who took Patrick away from Ireland?
3. Where did the ship Patrick sailed on eventually land?
4. How did God use Patrick to preserve the captain and many crew members?
5. Who were Patrick's first converts?
6. Where or to whom did the captain deliver the cargo and wolfhounds?

WORDS TO KNOW

trackless	fertile
authority	abundance
unruly	traveler
vicious	deposit

CHAPTER 11

A Divine Delay

The leader of the monks greeted Captain Noel in the Latin tongue and received little more than a nod. The captain knew little of the Latin language, but was wise enough to point the men in the direction of Patrick.

Although Patrick was a bit rusty in speaking Latin, he managed to converse well enough with the strangers. "You look like weary and hungry travelers," said Patrick, "how many days have you been on the road?"

"Almost thirty," said the middle-aged monk. "We could use a bit of fresh water and some food, do you know where any can be found?"

"A good spring and plenty of wild fruit trees are just over the horizon about two miles," asserted Patrick.

"Thank you friend!" bellowed the monk, whose name was Mark. "Where are you and your party bound?" he asked.

"The men here are going back to their ship which is docked at Burdigola. As for me," stated the former slave, "I wish to go wherever it is God's will."

"If you wish, come with us," Mark said. "We are going home to Auxerre. Our journey always seems shorter when it is made with good companions."

"Let me think on it for a time," said Patrick. "I will show you where to find a good place to camp this evening."

The monks smiled and walked ahead of Patrick and his new friend Mark. They were interested in getting to the spring and orchard before nightfall, and therefore, moved briskly down the country road. As Patrick and his companion walked along at their own pace, they talked about many things. Patrick told of his captivity, his escape, the trip with Noel, and his wonderful deliverance from near starvation. But Patrick was eager to hear about the condition of the Christian community in Gaul, so he finished his account as quickly as possible.

"Well," said the monk from Auxerre, "we are blessed to work alongside a godly bishop named Germanus, but most of the monks are preoccupied with superstitions instead of the Holy Scripture. Too many of our people forget that living in a monastery does not relieve the duty of God's people to take the message of the gospel into all of the world. Much of the Christian community in Gaul has received the Church of Rome, but not Christ; the sacraments, but not salvation; the bishops, but not the Mediator between God and man."

"Your honesty is like a breath of fresh air, my brother. I think that we will get along splendidly," said Patrick.

"Then you will journey with us to the monastery at Auxerre?" questioned the middle-aged monk.

"If only to help you pray for the needs of God's people in Gaul," responded Patrick enthusiastically.

As the afternoon turned into evening, the weary monks and their new traveling companion, reached the springs. These Christian brothers enjoyed the fresh water and lively fellowship and then made a quick excursion to the nearby orchards to get fruit and honey. Patrick was assured, more than once, that he would be welcomed by Bishop Germanus and the other Christians at the monastery.

"We welcome all travelers," said Mark, "and perhaps you too will be touched and influenced by the life and example of our great leader."

On they traveled through a fertile land that bloomed with fruit and sweet-smelling blossoms. Many joyful nights were spent by these servants of God, singing and praying around the campfire. Finally they reached the road that led up to the monastery at Auxerre. Several of the younger monks began to trot in the direction of their familiar dwelling, as they heard the bells ringing in the bell tower.

The entire group of men were warmly received by the head of the monastery, who was a great and learned scholar. Patrick felt humble and untutored in his presence. In spite of his embarrassment, the monks did everything in their power to make Patrick feel welcome.

It did not take long for Patrick to get into the routine of monastery life, which was, for the most part regulated by the ringing of bells. Four rings of the bell was the signal for morning prayer, five rings alerted the men that it was breakfast time, and so on. For this reason, Patrick found it easy to adapt himself to the kind of life led by the monks. For the first time since coming to faith in Christ, Patrick knew something of a peaceful life. Here in the monastery, the monks sought to lay aside what they considered to be the heavy burdens of ambitions, luxuries, and possessions. They had nothing of their own, sharing everything they had with one another, as they worked hard.

The older monks spent their time copying the Holy Scriptures by hand, for there were no printing presses at this time. It would take months for a skilled copyist to make even one copy of sacred Scripture. The younger men like Patrick worked in the fields during the day, and then spent long hours in prayer. All of the inhabitants of the monastery had but one meal a day and sometimes fasted.

Patrick found that many of the monks had been wealthy, vain, and sinful when they lived out in the world. Most of them had come to the monastery to find God and to live a simple life. Some monks found peace with their Maker and victory over their sinful passions as they came to faith in Christ. Other men who failed to find the Christ of Scripture while they lived in the monastery found only loneliness, sinful lusting, and frustration. Patrick was not exactly sure whether he would find the monastic life beneficial to him or not.

After Patrick had been at the monastery for three weeks, he finally had the opportunity to meet with Bishop Germanus. Both men shared a keen interest in the Word of God and loved to study the Scriptures. As a result, these Christian brothers got along very well from the start. The bishop was gracious enough to give Patrick a personal guided tour of the whole manuscript preparation operation that was in place at the monastery. Patrick marveled at the skill and diligence of the copyist and artists that worked on the copying of the Holy Scripture. In fact,

Patrick was so impressed by the leadership of Bishop Germanus that he decided to stay at the monastery until the Lord prompted him to leave.

Patrick soon became inspired to embark upon a diligent study of the Scriptures. His lengthy captivity in Ireland caused him to hunger for the Word of God. This holy exercise also helped him escape the dangers that are often associated with being idle of mind. He was seldom bored or needlessly tempted because his study of Scripture enabled him to constantly live with the thought of his Creator in his mind. Even though Patrick grew in his knowledge of God's Word, he often felt very ignorant as he worked alongside gifted scholars. After all, he had not been to school since he was fifteen. It was Patrick's intention to study hard to make up for the long, seemingly wasted years.

The weeks soon turned into months and before Patrick realized it, he had been a student at Auxerre for over two years. As the time passed, however, the former slave began to think more often of his distant home and aging parents. "Are my parents even alive?" was a question that com-

monly surfaced in his mind. These thoughts eventually
became very overwhelming to the young student. They
also became extremely perplexing, for Patrick had no idea
how he could reach Britain without a ship or money.

In the providence of God, a good friend of his and
fellow student named Clovus came one day to talk with
him. "I have been directed by my bishop to travel to Britain," said the excited classmate and monk. "This is a rare
opportunity for any of us, for we seldom have any business in Britain. Since you are from Britain, perhaps I can
persuade the bishop to let you join us?"

Patrick quickly agreed with the plan and sent his friend
on his way. A short time later, Patrick was thrilled to learn
that the bishop had approved his passage. Patrick's patience
was now being rewarded by Almighty God, and we can be
sure that this homesick young man was full of praise to his
merciful Lord.

Three days later, Clovus lead his little group of stu-
dents to a ship whose prow was pointed toward the coast
of Britain. Many years before,
Patrick had traveled on a
ship as a captive. Later he
had traveled on one as a
keeper of dogs.
Now he was trav-
eling as a free
man. He was
doubly pleased to
learn that their
destination was
near that part of
the coast where

Patrick had lived as a boy. He was filled with a mixture of joy and anxiety. Would he find his parents alive and well? He stood on deck waiting for the first sight of land.

On the fourth day, just as the sun was rising, a thin dark line in the distance grew more and more distinct, and now, Patrick could see the cliffs and hills he had known as a child. Falling on his knees, he cried out, "I thank Thee, dear Lord, for permitting me to see my home again."

COMPREHENSION QUESTIONS

1. What language did the monks speak?
2. Where did Mark take Patrick?
3. What type of activities did the monks engage in at the monastery?
4. Why did many of the men join the monastery?
5. Who was the bishop in charge of the monastery at Auxerre?
6. How did Patrick obtain passage to his homeland?

WORDS TO KNOW

distinct	embark
passage	inspired
overwhelm	monastery
seldom	manuscript

CHAPTER 12

Home at Last

As soon as the ship reached the shore, Patrick said farewell to his friend Clovus, and hurried off to the village of Bannavem. But when he reached the village, he immediately noticed that it was not the same as when he left eight years before. The mighty wall that had formerly protected the town had been torn down. New houses and shops had been built. Only the meeting place of the council seemed the same. Patrick decided to pay a visit to the council building in hopes that his father might be there.

The members of the council, who were just ending a meeting, gazed curiously at the tall young man who stood before them. Then one of them uttered a cry of amazement.

"Are you little Patricius?" he asked.

"I am," said Patrick smiling.

He threw his arms around Patrick and cried. "We thought you were dead!"

Members of the council gathered around the young man who had seemingly come back from the dead. As they greeted Patrick, they saw in the strong adult signs of the fifteen-year-old boy they had once seen playing with their own children.

"What news have you of my mother and father?" asked Patrick to the assembly at Bannavem.

"Thanks be to God," said one of the council members. "Your folks are safe at home. Your father is growing old, however, and cannot always attend council meetings like he used to years ago."

"I understand," responded Patrick, "can someone lend me a horse so I can travel swiftly to my old home?"

"Certainly," said an elderly council member. "You may take any of the horses that are saddled in the barn across the way."

Several minutes later, Patrick was galloping down the road which lead out of Bannavem. He was amazed to discover how much of the old landscape he still remembered as the miles passed quickly by. Before long, the long-lost son could see the cottages and barns that he used to call home. At long last, Patrick would be able to look upon his honored parents and take his place once again on his father's lands.

As the sun rose high in the sky, Patrick finally trotted up to the barns which were close to his parents cottage. After he dismounted, a voice called out to him from the direction of the sea. Moments later, Patrick could see his mother and father moving swiftly across the yard with amazed looks on their faces.

"Son, Son, is that really you?" cried Calpornius, "I can hardly believe my eyes!"

Patrick was so filled with emotion and excitement that he could not speak. He decided to give his parents a long hug and then kneeled down before his father. As soon as Patrick regained his composure, he asked his father to forgive him for failing to diligently watch out for raiders and for missing the opportunity to warn the people of Bannavem of approaching danger.

"You have nothing to apologize for, Son," said Calpornius as he fought back his tears. "I have never doubted that on that dark day many years ago, you did your best. Now arise, Son, and know that your mother and father receive you back with joy and thankfulness in our hearts to God."

Patrick stood up and walked slowly across the yard with his parents side by side. They had so much to talk about, so much to catch up on, that they hardly knew where to begin. After a few moments of silence, Patrick's

Patrick's parents lived on a small farm near Dumbarton, Pictland

mother stated, "You must be tired and hungry after your long ride, why don't we step inside the cottage for a warm meal."

"Grand idea, Mother," said Patrick gratefully. "I could use a bite to eat and a short rest."

After Patrick awoke from his rest, he soon realized that he had slept a long time for the morning sun was just beginning to rise in the sky. Patrick washed up and changed his clothes before coming out to visit with his parents once again. "I suppose that I was more tired than I realized," said the mildly embarrassed son as he walked into the living room.

"Don't be embarrassed, Son," said Calpornius, "we figured that you would probably sleep through the night." He then added, "What is it that you wish to do with yourself Patricius?"

"Why, work with you on the farm for a season," responded Patrick in a sleepy tone. "By the way, does Mother still serve breakfast around this place?"

"Yes, yes I do," uttered Conchesa as she entered into the conversation. "And if you know what's good for you, Son, you will eat heartily for Father undoubtedly has a dozen chores for his not-so-little boy."

As the three sat around the breakfast table, they talked about many things. For the most part, however, they talked about what had happened to each other during the years of separation. Patrick's parents were understandably thrilled to hear how God had brought their son into a living relationship with Jesus Christ, and how He preserved him through many trials. Calpornius in turn was delighted to tell Patrick about how the Lord miraculously preserved them from the raiders and from many difficulties. For the first time, these family members could praise the Lord together.

After breakfast was over, Patrick and his father decided to work together. Gale force winds had damaged the thatched roof on the old barn and Calpornius was eager to repair it before further damage was done. As the men began to work, Patrick continued to ask many questions about what had happened to Britain during the time he was away. His father informed him of the fact that the Roman Empire was beginning to crumble. The once proud Roman legions had abandoned their occupation of Britain and showed no signs of returning. As a result, the people of Britain were finally learning how to protect and rule over themselves.

What neither Patrick nor his father realized, however, was that this process of change was really the birth of a new nation that would eventually be called England. In time, this nation would become mighty, even to the extent of ruling over Ireland and Scotland, because the British people were released from the yoke of Roman rule.

For several months, Patrick lived at the old farmhouse and enjoyed a relatively peaceful and comfortable life. As the days passed swiftly by, the long-lost slave soon fell into the routine of a common farmhand. Calpornius was happy to see that his son was adjusting very well to his new duties. He hoped that someday, Patrick would take over his estate and walk in his footsteps.

In the providence of God, however, the young man named Patrick was, once again, becoming restless in his spirit. For reasons which he could not fully grasp, Patrick was starting to discern that God did not intend for him to live out his days as a comfortable landowner. At first, Patrick tried to fight against the prompting of the Lord and worked hard to give his parents the impression that he was home for good. This effort, however, eventually became more and more difficult for the former slave to maintain.

Patrick had been home nearly a year when he experienced an unusual and unexpected dream that had spiritual significance. One night while Patrick was dreaming, he had a vision of a man from Ireland named Victoricus who came toward him carrying many letters. This man

gave one of the letters to Patrick who read the opening
words, which were, "The voice of the Irish." At the same
moment, he thought that he heard the Irish people calling
out, "We beg you, holy youth, to come and walk among
us once more." As soon as Patrick heard these words, he
was heartbroken and could read no further. In fact, the
words disturbed him so much that he immediately awoke
from his sleep.

The next day, Patrick summoned the
courage to speak to his father about
his strange vision and dream. He
began by asking his dad, "Father, have you ever had visions
in the night?"

"Well, I have had very
detailed and realistic
dreams on several occa-
sions," admitted Calpornius,
"but then again, we do know that God sometimes com-
municates to his servants through dreams or visions."

"Yes, but to what degree should we follow such things?"
questioned the perplexed son. "I want to do God's will,
but how do I know that this message is from the Lord?"

"You must study the Scriptures and pray for the wisdom to discern God's will for your life," responded
Calpornius. "Be patient, Son, and continue to wait upon
the Lord. In time, you will know if this dream is truly
from the Lord or is just an empty message. Never forget
that the Holy Scripture contains the only reliable form of
divine revelation known to man."

"I cannot disagree with your counsel, Father," said
Patrick. "Besides, I still need to learn a great deal more about

the Word of God before I can go forth as a missionary."

"To tell you the truth, Son," added Calpornius, "I have been a deacon for many years with the church at Dumbarton and I still feel unqualified to serve as a missionary. If you ask me, it would be just as well to forget the people of Ireland. The Celtic clans over there are fierce and barbaric."

"I will try to be patient and to broaden my education Father," said Patrick, "but I doubt that God will let me forget about my calling to the Irish people."

COMPREHENSION QUESTIONS

1. How did Patrick travel from Bannavem to his father's farm?
2. What did Calpornius tell his son about the condition of the Roman empire?
3. What did Patrick's father wish he would do with his future?
4. Who was Victoricus?
5. What message did Victoricus leave with Patrick?
6. What advice did Calpornius give Patrick regarding his vision in the night?

WORDS TO KNOW

counsel	yoke
barbaric	embarrass
deacon	loan
preserved	landscape

CHAPTER 13

Training for Service

As additional weeks slipped by, Patrick found that
he was, at least, correct about one issue. God would
not permit the words and plea of the Irish people
to be forgotten. Every few days, the Lord would cause something to be said or done that would bring to Patrick's mind
the needs of the lost in Ireland. The more Patrick considered God's will for his life through prayer and Bible study,
the more he became convinced that he had to leave his
comfortable home. He had to get better prepared to reach
out to the Irish people, and that meant going away for
further education and training.

All of these thoughts seemed well and fine, and yet,
Patrick knew very well that he might break his parents'
heart if he left them once again. For days, Patrick agonized
about how to break the news to his mother and father. At
times, he was not even sure if God truly wanted him to
leave his aging parents. It was not until Patrick came across
the words of Jesus as found in the Book of Matthew, that
he finally felt at peace about his position. Patrick read a
passage from the tenth chapter of Matthew, beginning at
the thirty-seventh verse that stated, "He that loveth father
or mother more than me is not worthy of me: and he that
loveth son or daughter more than me is not worthy of me.

And he that taketh not his cross, and followeth after me, is not worthy of me."

As expected, Patrick's parents were not pleased to hear of their son's decision to leave home once again. In fact, they pleaded with him to stay and help out around the farm. "Haven't we treated you with love and honor since your return?" asked Patrick's mother.

"Of course, mother," pleaded Patrick, "But my life is not my own. You of all women must know that I must do the will of my Heavenly Father first and always. And God has directed me to serve Him on distant shores."

Calpornius sat quietly as his son and wife exchanged heartfelt concerns and at least a little anxiety. Finally, he said, "Listen, both of you, to my words. As hard as it is to let go of a treasured son, it at least causes me to remember how God himself must have felt when He gave His only begotten Son to a lost and sinful world. We will support your decision, my son, and help you to find your place in God's world."

From that moment on, Patrick received nothing but support from his parents. His father even gave him letters of introduction which Patrick could use during his initial visit with the bishop of the Celtic church in London. Unlike pagan Ireland, there was a rapidly growing Christian church among the Celts who lived in Britain and Pictland.

"I advise you to petition the Synod in the south of Britain to appoint you to a good mission school or to be tutored by a gifted scholar," said Calpornius to his devoted son.

"Very well, Father," said Patrick, "I will talk with the bishop and the Synod members as soon as I arrive in London."

A month later, Patrick was on a ship heading toward

the southeastern corner of Britain. He had stayed at home long enough to help his father put his property and herds in good order. Now, however, he was finished with his farewells and was enjoying an uneventful voyage at sea.

Several days later, the ship reached port and the young man from Bannavem found transport on a wagon heading towards London. As Patrick rode along the bumpy road, he enjoyed looking at the pretty farms and wild animals of the forest. He was certainly glad to have found a way to get to London that did not involve much walking. Patrick had two large trunks with him, and this made it difficult for him to travel long distances by foot.

After several days in transit, Patrick finally arrived in the town of London. Although London was not at this time nearly as large a city as it is today, it was still very large by Patrick's standards. Upon arriving at this location, Patrick's first goal was to find out where the bishop had his residence. He stopped several local citizens before one of them finally gave him the directions he needed.

The people of London who looked upon Patrick must have been tempted to laugh. This young lad was at the end of a long journey and had wrinkled clothes, ruffled hair, and was dragging two large trunks behind him. At this point, Patrick probably did not care who laughed at him.

He was on a mission to find the bishop of the Christian church in London and his only concern was to complete that task.

After stopping for a brief period to rest, Patrick finally reached the residence of the bishop. The first person he met was Lawrence, a big, cheerful man about his own age. And the first words he heard were "Welcome, stranger," spoken by Lawrence in Patrick's native Latin tongue.

The youthful visitor from Bannavem was immediately taken to the bishop's study where he sat down and spoke with him at length. Halfway through their conversation, Patrick invited the bishop to read the letter of introduction that he had brought from his father. Patrick found it easy to talk freely with the leader of the Celtic church in London and told him everything that was on his heart concerning ministry preparation. When he had finished his story, he added humbly that he was badly in need of further training and that he had come to the South of Britain hoping to learn more about the teachings of Scripture.

"I think we can help you, Patrick," said the bishop of London. "It will be hard work. You must learn everything that Christ Himself taught us while He was on earth. You will not find it easy. But," the bishop added with a smile, "I think you will also find that there are patient, sympathetic teachers among us."

In the months that followed, Patrick's learning experiences were numerous and varied. For several weeks, the young student was sent to a small village on the outskirts of London to be trained by a local pastor who was a scholar. Later, he traveled with a Celtic evangelist on a short-term missionary trip to Gaul. Patrick studied as he had never studied before, and the more he studied, the greater was his hunger for learning.

As the years passed, Patrick was elected to the office of deacon for a small Celtic church in the southwestern part of Britain. He served the church in this region for over a year, while he continued to further his education. On many occasions, Patrick submitted an appeal to the bishop for an appointment as a missionary to the Irish people. Each request, however, was denied because the bishop felt that the Celtic church in Ireland was so weak that it could not prevent British missionaries from becoming martyrs.

Although it was difficult for Patrick to fight off his anxious feelings, he found the grace to wait upon the Lord's perfect timing. Patrick had now been gone from his home in Bannavem for ten years and had established himself as a faithful deacon and hard-working scholar. He had finally lost the boyish look of his youth and was a mature man of God—both physically and spiritually.

It was at this season of Patrick's life that God began to reward him for his patience and faithfulness. While Patrick was in the vicinity of London ministering to the needs of needy Christians, he received a call from the bishop to attend a synod meeting. This meeting of church leaders was set for the following week and Patrick soon discovered, much to his delight, that church leaders from throughout Britain were being summoned to hear from a delegation that had just returned from Ireland.

When the church leaders were assembled, Noran, the leader of the Irish delegation, made his plea. He said that there were hundreds of genuine believers in Ireland, but they, as scattered sheep, were not powerful enough to combat the kings and Druids. He pleaded with the council to send a bishop to Ireland who could lead the Christians who were sowing the gospel in tears so that they might reap in joy. They needed a man who would act upon the Great Commission in a bold and decisive manner.

Patrick sat listening to this in great excitement. Was this finally the moment when God would permit him to preach the Gospel to the people of God in Ireland? He had never forgotten the vision of the man Victoricus who brought letters from the voice of the Irish crying out, "We beg you, holy youth, to come and walk among us once more."

As Patrick sat there in silence, he listened to the leaders of the Celtic church discussing the worthiness of supporting a mission work in Ireland. One leader after another voiced concerns or objections to the proposal. Some of the men stressed the high costs of such a mission and the dangers involved to church personnel working among savage pagan tribes. Other leaders were quick to question whether the church in Britain should expand its effort to evangelize foreign lands, when it seemed as though their own local churches were so small and weak. Just when it seemed that the proposal was about to be voted down, the not-so-young deacon from Bannavem slowly rose to speak.

"Esteemed bishops and friends," said Patrick, "I beg you to give me a hearing in regard to this matter of Ireland. Our brother in Christ, Noran, has shared his burden for his downcast people. I also share this burden and feel compelled to exhort you to consider anew what Christ has commanded His church to do and be. We must never forget that Christ has commissioned us to go into all the world and teach all nations, baptizing them in the name of the Father, Son, and Holy Spirit. We must, therefore, in spite of difficult obstacles, be willing to boldly let our light shine before men in other parts of God's world."

"Yes," admitted a bishop who was sitting close by, "but sometimes the people we need to reach the most are in our own backyard."

"I will not try to argue with that point," responded Patrick thoughtfully. "All that I can do is to testify to the fact that God calls some men to serve Him in foreign lands. I truly believe that I am one such man, dear brother."

"Are you telling us Deacon Patrick, that you are willing to preach to savage pagans in Ireland?" questioned the curious bishop.

"Yes," said Patrick plainly to a somewhat surprised audience.

As these two men finished their dialog, the moderator of the meeting recommended that a decision regarding the Ireland question be postponed until their next session. This recommendation was promptly passed by the synod members who closed their meeting in prayer a short time later.

Later that same evening, Patrick was approached by the bishop of London regarding the comments he made during the meeting. "I have discussed your position with several council members, Patrick," said the bishop, "and I would like to speak with you further about establishing a mission to Ireland."

"I would like nothing better," replied Patrick gratefully.

Two days later, Patrick walked into the study of the bishop of London and sat in front of a roaring fire. As he sat waiting for the bishop, he could not help but wonder what God had in store for him. He was trying not to get his hopes up too high, and yet, he was troubled to think about how many years he had already waited to serve God in Ireland. While the would-be missionary thought on these things, his spiritual leader walked into the room.

"Greetings in the precious name of Jesus," said the bishop of London. "Thank you for coming as requested Deacon Patrick."

After a few moments of silence the bishop added, "One look at you, my friend, makes me think that you are weighted down in your spirit. Is this Ireland issue at the heart of it?"

"I am in truth troubled in my spirit," admitted Patrick. "Over the last several years, I have labored at serving the practical needs of my local church and in my study of Scripture to be the man God would have me be. But now, I am burdened with guilt because I know the Lord has called me to be a missionary to Ireland and yet I stay here."

"Even missionaries need time to study and make spiritual preparations for the mission field, Patrick," remarked the bishop.

"True enough," uttered the troubled Deacon as he rose from his seat. "But it has been ten years since I came among you and still my bags are not packed for the mission field. You see," continued Patrick, "my conscience is held captive to the clear call that I have been given to go back to Ireland. The Lord simply will not permit me to turn aside from this missionary outreach. It is very strange, indeed, that God would call someone as unqualified as me to represent the gospel before the Irish people. Nevertheless, my duty is to obey the promptings of the Holy Spirit as those promptings harmonize with Scripture, and God will not give me peace until I obey. As the Apostle Paul once said to the church at Corinth, 'woe is unto me, if I preach not the gospel.'"

"I had no idea how great your burden was, dear brother," confessed the leader of the church in London. "Under the circumstances it is imperative that you not stay in Britain any longer than is necessary. I will speak to the council on your behalf, and see if they will release you to the mission field of Ireland."

"Thank you for giving me a hearing, Bishop," uttered the grateful Patrick. "My primary desire is to gain your blessing on my work before departing," he added. "As to the issue of authority, I go to serve the church in Ireland under the authority of Jesus Christ alone."

"As you wish my son," responded the bishop. "I will still seek the blessing of the council on your behalf and will do what I can to arrange passage for you and a servant at all speed."

Patrick thanked the bishop once again and proceeded to make his way back to the home where he was staying. The next morning, Patrick decided to return to the city of Canterbury to await the decision of the synod. Two months passed before he finally received a letter from the archbishop.

The long awaited letter was delivered to Patrick by a young messenger, who found him studying in a church library at the monastery in Canterbury. Patrick thanked the young man and proceeded to read the lengthy letter. Much to his surprise, the official correspondence informed him that the synod had recently met and decided in favor of establishing a missionary work in Ireland. The letter went on to say that the council of bishops had also voted to ordain him as a bishop to the Celtic church in Ireland. This move, explained the bishop, was to ensure that he would have the authority that was necessary to influence the independently-minded church leaders in Ireland.

Patrick read the letter several times to make sure he was not dreaming. It did not take long, however, for him to realize that he was receiving an answer to prayer. The closing paragraph of the official correspondence that he received, directed him to appear in London the following month to be ordained and installed as bishop to the church in Ireland.

Patrick could not sleep that night. He decided, therefore, to spend the long hours of the night praying to God for strength and wisdom. As Patrick fell on his knees, his heart was filled with joy and simple, child-like faith. This humble Christian prayed that God would bless his preparations to minister to the Irish people.

The time soon arrived for Patrick to be ordained. A solemn assembly of bishops met in a stone church located on the outskirts of London to perform the ordination service. Shortly after the service, Patrick had the opportunity to meet with the two men who had been appointed to travel with him on the mission field. The new bishop of Ireland was greatly impressed with the men that had been assigned to him and was anxious to let these men prove their worth.

After a good night's sleep, the three men rode south together in an old cart, pulled by a sturdy horse. Patrick and his new aid Kent sat in the back of the cart while a man named Arin sat in front and guided the horse. Mile after mile passed on until the three brothers in Christ finally reached a small town on the coast of England.

The final preparations took several weeks. A ship was outfitted and loaded with all the supplies Patrick would need. He hoped to build many churches in Ireland, so he took a number of tools with him in addition to his other supplies. The most precious cargo that Patrick stowed aboard the ship, were his copies of the Holy Scripture and his maps of the land of Ireland.

Finally the great day arrived, and Patrick and his little company obeyed the voice of the captain to board the ship and make ready for sail. As the small vessel floated out into deeper water, Patrick whispered a prayer from his heart, "May God make His face to shine upon us."

COMPREHENSION QUESTIONS

1. How did Patrick finally gain a peaceful attitude about leaving home?
2. What did Calpornius give his son to use during his visit with the bishop?
3. How did Patrick travel to the city of London?
4. How did the bishop help Patrick after he arrived in London?
5. What office was Patrick elected to in his local church?
6. Who came from Ireland to speak to the assembly of British bishops?

WORDS TO KNOW

tutor	transport
appoint	martyr
preparation	delegation
initial	obstacle

CHAPTER 14

Pulling Down Stronghold

I t took four days for the ship which was carrying the new Bishop of Ireland to reach the harbor at Inverdea. The weather had been fair and the winds favorable to the captain and crew. The spot where Patrick landed was situated at the mouth of the Varty River in County Wicklow. This was the very place from which Patrick had escaped many years before.

As soon as the ship was safely anchored in the harbor, Patrick and his men were rowed ashore. It took several minutes for them to unload their trunks and supplies. The farmers from the local area were kind enough to offer to store the items that Patrick's team had brought with them. These men were apparently part of the tiny host of believers who were living along the east coast of Ireland.

Patrick, Kent, and Arin were eager to meet the local chieftain to present the truth of the gospel to him. It was Patrick's belief that if he could convert the leader of the local clan, he would have an open door to reach many people throughout the region. Therefore, Patrick asked one of the local farmers if he knew the best way to get in touch with the chieftain of his area.

"I am not sure if it is wise for me to tell you," stated the farmer in his simple Gaelic tongue. "The last bishop to visit this region, a man named Palladius, had ties with Rome but that did not help him get along well with our chieftain. In fact, this bishop barely lasted a year in our midst before he was chased out by the king's warriors a year ago.

"I am not a bishop from Rome," responded Patrick. "I come under the direction of the Celtic church in Britain and by the authority of Jesus Christ alone. My mission is one of peace, I desire to lead the Irish kings and people to saving faith in the Lord of earth and heaven."

The farmer explained that Dunbar was the chieftain of the region. "But I am afraid that this ruler will not allow you to stay," added the poor farmer sadly. "It may be best for you and your men to move out of this area quickly."

As they talked, a group of armed men approached. They looked fierce with their long hair, heavy beards, and gleaming swords. Their leader stepped forward, and upon recognizing the old farmer, asked him. "Who are these strangers?"

"This is Bishop Patrick, and the others are holy men who have come on a peaceful mission to lead the people of Ireland to God," responded the farmer nervously.

"I am Garric," the leader of the armed men told Patrick. "I am the son of Dunbar, and I order you to leave here by nightfall."

The new bishop said calmly, "I was on my way to see you and your father to ask if I might stay in your province awhile."

"No, you cannot," Garric said sternly. "I allowed Palladius to stay here for a short time and he caused nothing but trouble. We have enough problems with the followers of the Christian God, and the mighty Dunbar is very angry with people like you who steer the people away from the Druid priests. He has given me orders to arrest and kill Christian leaders like you on the spot."

Patrick remained calm, saying gently, "If it be God's will that I am to die even before I have begun my work here, then, O Prince, draw your sword and obey the orders of your father."

For a moment no one spoke. Garric's right hand fell upon the hilt of his heavy sword. He took a step forward. Then he said, "If I were to kill you, holy man, my wife would never forgive me. But leave now, before my father hears of your arrival."

With heaviness of heart, Patrick ordered his men to purchase a cart for their belongings. "We will move north toward Dublin," said the bishop confidently. "As it says in the Holy Scriptures, if they will not receive you in one village, shake the dust off of your feet, and move on to the next."

The next morning, the three missionaries found themselves in the middle of the countryside several miles away from Dublin. "Let us walk to the top of the hill that I see a mile away," Patrick said. "From there we can see all of this part of the country."

As they walked toward the hill, they saw a group of men waiting there. Then the silence of the morning was shattered by the angry growling of dogs. The sound struck terror in the hearts of Patrick's companions. Moments later, four dogs rushed down that hill toward the defenseless men who carried no swords or weapons.

Patrick stood there calmly while the others dropped to their knees in fright. "Surely," they thought, "these wild dogs will tear us to bits." The dogs—huge, fierce Irish wolfhounds—were snarling as they rushed toward Patrick and his group of frightened men. Then Patrick's clear voice rang out. He talked to these wolfhounds as he had once talked to the dogs which had helped him guard sheep on the Slemish Mountains. As soon as the dogs heard the familiar commands in a language they understood, they stopped snarling. A short time later, Patrick gave a sharp command and the wolfhounds halted in their tracks. Patrick then proceeded to walk toward the dogs, talking soothingly to them. The dogs dropped to the ground. They whimpered and crawled toward Patrick, and then they arose and licked his outstretched hand.

The men on the hill had watched all this in amazement. Among them was Dunbar, the king, who had taught the dogs to kill his enemies. To Dunbar, any strangers who landed on his shores were to be treated as enemies. But Dunbar now had to face up to the fact that his newest "enemy" held as much control over his own hounds as himself.

He led his men down the hill and approached the three strangers. "Who are you?" he asked loudly.

Patrick answered his question and also told him why he had come to Ireland.

"But don't you know, Patrick," Dunbar said, "that many kings in Ireland have vowed to kill you if you are indeed the one spoken of in the prophecy?"

Patrick nodded. "Of course, I have heard of your Irish prophecies, but I have faith in God to protect his servants."

"Do you believe that your Christian God can protect you against the swords of Irish kings?" Dunbar asked.

A small grin came across Patrick's face. "That is a small thing for the Creator of Heaven and Earth to do," he responded.

"I know very little about your God," Dunbar admitted. "I should like to know more about such a God. Will you and your band stay with me awhile, and will you tell me of this God of yours?"

Patrick accepted the invitation, and he and his helpers were housed in Dunbar's castle. Every day Dunbar sat and listened as Patrick told of the miracles Jesus had performed and of His power to change the hearts of sinful men.

Sitting with the king and listening to the stories was Dunbar's older brother, Ronus. "Many years ago," began Dunbar, "my brother was wounded in battle and captured by a Druid priest from an unfriendly clan. This priest pronounced a curse upon the young warrior that was so powerful that he has never been able to recover his mind. Even to this day, many of our people believe that he is demon possessed. Is your God powerful enough to undo the curse of a Druid priest?"

"I cannot force God to deliver your brother from the power of demons, but this I know, if humble creatures like us desire something we must have the faith to ask confidently. I will be glad to fast and pray for your brother to be saved from the powers of darkness," said Patrick sincerely.

Then Patrick put his hand upon the head of Ronus, closed his eyes, and asked God to give the old warrior freedom from demons and a new life in Christ. Suddenly there was a sharp cry from the brother of the king. His face lit up as though the early morning sun was shining on it, and for the first time in years, he actually smiled.

"I don't know what is happening, Dunbar," said the old warrior joyfully. "All I know is that my heart became peaceful as soon as I prayed to this Jesus that Patrick kept talking about." Stepping forward, Ronus embraced Patrick, as tears rolled down his cheeks. "You have given me back my mind, Patrick," he cried.

"Not I," said Patrick correcting him. "It was God who did this. He had some purpose in giving you your health. I trust that He will guide you as you serve Him as Lord and Savior."

"I believe I already know what must be done now," said Ronus clearly. "You have told my brother many things about the way of salvation and the importance of baptism. I plead with you, Patrick, teach me more about this Jesus so I can be baptized."

"And while you are at it, bishop," said Dunbar, the king, "you may baptize me as well, I want to be part of the Christian faith. I am tired of worshipping false gods. You have come among us unarmed and you have shown us the true and living God—the Prince of peace. In thanksgiving, holy Patrick, let us sacrifice to the true God."

The new bishop of Ireland explained that the only sacrifice acceptable to God was a broken and contrite spirit, one which humbly accepts the sacrifice of Christ on the cross as being complete and sufficient to cancel out sin's penalty.

"Is there nothing that I can do besides this to show my gratefulness to the Lord for delivering my people from darkness?" asked Dunbar.

"If you wish to help me let the light of the Gospel shine in your realm, King Dunbar," said Patrick, "then let's build the first Christian church in Ireland on that hill over there. For reasons already explained, dear brother, our church will not need an altar—only a solid foundation, sound roof, and a simple wooden or stone cross."

"I would be happy to have my men build a new church building, Bishop," responded the excited king.

Patrick nodded and led the little assembly in prayer for those who were converted and for the church building project. After he finished his prayer, he turned to his faithful servant, Kent, and asked, "Are you ready to serve the Lord in this place and shepherd the lambs that God sends into your midst?"

For a moment, Kent was speechless. Finally, he was able to respond and said, "Are you asking me to stay here and lead the work of the church in this place?"

"Yes, my brother," said Patrick plainly. "You have the gifts and the heart to faithfully water what has been planted here. I desire you to feed this people with the Law of God and the message of Christ."

"I have come to Ireland to assist you in the spreading of the Christian faith, dear bishop," said Kent, "if you, therefore, wish me to serve here, I will do so cheerfully."

Patrick gave a firm hug to his brother, Kent, and walked back towards the castle with the others. Within three weeks, a small church building, complete with a stone cross, stood firmly on the hill which overlooked Dunbar's castle. By God's grace, Patrick was able to establish the first foothold for the gospel in the wild and dangerous mission field of Ireland.

COMPREHENSION QUESTIONS

1. Where did the new bishop to Ireland first come ashore?
2. What was the name of Dunbar's son?
3. Who was Dunbar?
4. What problem did God take away from Ronus?
5. What did Dunbar build for Patrick?
6. Who did Patrick leave as a minister to Dunbar's realm?

WORDS TO KNOW

midst	invitation
sufficient	curse
unarmed	vowed
demon	nightfall

A Mission to Tara

Patrick stayed for several weeks in the vicinity of King Dunbar's castle, preaching to a number of visitors and training his friend, Kent, to be an effective pastor. When the people learned that Dunbar and his brother had become Christians, they came to listen to Patrick as he preached the gospel of Jesus Christ. Every week, the new bishop of Ireland baptized more and more converts. Then he told Dunbar that it was time for him to move on.

"But who will teach our people about Jesus?" the king asked anxiously. "There are hundreds here who will join the faith I have embraced if only they can hear you."

"As I have told your brother, I shall leave my assistant Kent here to be your minister," Patrick promised. "He is well trained and a faithful servant of Christ. His knowledge of Scripture is, in many ways, better than my own. By God's grace, he will keep alive the spark of faith that the Holy Spirit has ignited here."

"But where will you go, Patrick?" Dunbar asked.

"I shall go to Tara and confront the king there," Patrick said simply.

"You must not, you cannot!" cried Dunbar. "Loegaire is the High King of Tara, and Lochru is his chief Druid. For years, both have been afraid of the ancient prophecy regarding a Christian deliverer. If you go to Tara, they will have you put to death."

"I was at Tara once before," Patrick reminded him, "and I was not put to death."

"Yes, but Nial of the Nine Hostages was king then," Dunbar said. "Loegaire is his son, and he is a cruel man."

"That may be," Patrick conceded, "but I must go. As you say, he is the most powerful king in all Ireland. If he will give me leave to preach in Tara, I feel I can do much to extend God's kingdom throughout Ireland."

The next day, Patrick, Arin, and three servants from Dunbar's castle started south for Tara, but the news of their coming was already known to Lochru and his wicked brother, Lucetmal. These Druids had spies everywhere who had brought to Tara word of how Patrick had converted Dunbar and many of his followers. They also learned of how Dunbar had been persuaded to build a place for Christian worship. After learning that Patrick was on his way to Tara, the two Druids hurried to Loegaire with the information they had gathered.

"This man is coming, O King, to defy you and our ancient gods," Lochru said. "He must be slain before he upsets the holy feast of Beltain" (pronounced *Beltine*).

"When he arrives here," the king said angrily, "watch everything he does and report to me. If he does anything to offend me or our gods, he shall surely die."

Meanwhile, Patrick, Arin, and the others were making their way slowly toward Tara. One afternoon they stopped before the house of a friendly peasant. The man of the house, who was the local carpenter, was kind enough to invite them inside for a meal. Patrick and his band accepted the invitation with pleasure. Soon they were eating good food and drinking fresh milk. They were about to finish their meal when the carpenter asked, "What brings you into this part of the country, strangers?"

Arin responded, "We are on our way to see King Loegaire."

"O you are," stated the gracious host. "You men don't look like the type to take part in a Druid festival. Then again," he added, "maybe you are just like many Irish people who like to view the huge bonfire that opens the feast of Beltain."

"Bonfire, Feast of Beltain, these words mean nothing to strangers like us," said Arin. "What is all this about?" questioned the young pilgrim.

"Well, young man, I am talking about an old Druid custom that is designed to honor the High King at Tara. Every year at this time," said the friendly carpenter, "each person living around Tara is commanded to cease from lighting any fires, upon penalty of death. During the evening just prior to the Druid festival, the High King has the honor of lighting a huge bonfire, which symbolizes the power of the king and the Druids over the powers of darkness. King Loegaire takes great pride in this act."

"How interesting that this pagan feast comes at the same period as our traditional celebration of the Resurrection of Christ," commented Patrick as he quietly listened at the dinner table. "I believe I know how to get an audience with the king," added the bishop of Ireland as he fought back a grin.

"Just what is going on inside that head of yours, Patrick?" questioned Arin. "You are not thinking of provoking a confrontation with violent King Loegaire are you?" asked the nervous missionary.

"I would not suggest such a plan, dear friend," added the carpenter. "This king will kill anyone who tries to rob him of his glory."

"Only one King is truly worthy of glory," mentioned Patrick, "and that is the King of Glory—the Lord Jesus Christ. It is to Him that I will raise the largest bonfire in these parts tomorrow night, just a short distance from the castle at Tara."

"Suit yourself," said the host as he shook his head, "I hope this God of yours is as powerful as you say."

"He is indeed," said the bishop confidently.

One hour later, Patrick led the way toward the castle at Tara, where Loegaire was king. They crossed the River Boyne and walked to the top of the Hill of Slane. This hill was only two miles away from the region known as Tara.

"Tomorrow is Resurrection Sunday," Patrick reminded his little band. "We shall hold services here on this hill. But now let us build a mighty pile of logs and sticks for our celebration tonight. We will let the whole region know that Jesus is the true Light of the world!"

"Dear Bishop," Arin warned, laying his hand on his friend's shoulder, "what you are doing now is to declare war on the High King of Ireland."

Patrick shook his head. "No, Arin, I am declaring war

on false gods, on ignorance, and on the Druids."

As the sun began to set, Loegaire, his two chief Druids, and all of the court were assembled outside the same great hall where Patrick had been sold into slavery as a boy. They were in the process of making their way to the woods to begin their pa-  gan ceremonies when they noticed a light in the distance. Moments later, the assembly looked upon the flames of a mighty fire that had been started by Patrick. The fire was so bright that it lit up the sky.

"Who is it who dares defy our laws?" King Loegaire shouted angrily. Lochru said, "It is Patrick, of whom I told you. He is challenging our authority. Unless we destroy him, the fire he has lit will overcome all the fires of our religion. And he who has kindled this fire will overcome us all and you too, O King."

"Go get him," the king commanded angrily, "and bring him here."

The two Druids climbed into a chariot and ordered twenty armed warriors to go with them. The sounds of chariot wheels and pounding hoofs were soon heard on the narrow road that led up the slope of the Hill of Slane. Patrick stood calmly near his bonfire as Lochru stepped out of his chariot.

"Our great king demands your presence," he said angrily. "You have broken our laws and defied our gods."

"Well of course I have. Your gods are worthless," Patrick said fearlessly.

"Get yourself and your men into the chariots," Lochru ordered.

"Some men put their trust in chariots and some put their trust in horses," Patrick smiled. "But we will walk, in the name of the Lord our God, to meet your king."

So Patrick and his men walked behind the chariots to the great hall of Tara. Lochru motioned them to enter. Loegaire sat where his father Nial had sat so many years before, at the head of the long table. All his chieftains, nobles, and warriors sat around it. They remained seated as Patrick and his band walked to the middle of the hall. Then, surprisingly, one of them—a young man—arose and bowed to Patrick.

"Welcome, Patrick," he said. "My name is Eric."

Patrick raised his hand and blessed this brave youth, while all others remained seated. Then the King asked Patrick in an angry tone, "How dare you defy Ireland's king?"

The bishop of Ireland calmly responded, "I came to Tara to ask your permission to do my work in the fairest of all lands. My mission is a peaceful one, brave King. If my work threatens any party, it is the Druids."

"What exactly is your work?" the king asked.

"It is God's work," Patrick said, "not the work of the false gods whom your Druids have taught you to worship, but the work of the only true God, Who is our Father in heaven."

The king turned to Lucetmal. "Before we condemn this man to death for his sacrilege," he said bluntly, "question him about this strange God of his."

"Who is your God?" Lucetmal shouted. "And where does He live?"

"He is Jesus Christ," Patrick said, "and He lives everywhere."

"Has he any sons?" Lucetmal sneered.

"The Lord Jesus has many children," responded Patrick, "everyone who forsakes his own wicked ways and trusts in the mercy and grace of Christ can be his son or daughter."

"Is He a young God?"

"He is older than the oldest man alive, and yet he never grows old," Patrick said. "He has no age. He has always been, and He always will be, and He will live forever."

"What did your God ever do to make Him so important?" the Druid wanted to know.

"He created Heaven and Earth," said the bishop of Ireland. "He created man in His own image. He is God the Father, God the Son, and God the Holy Spirit. The one true God is made up of three Persons—called the Godhead or the Holy Trinity."

"This is truly silly," the Druid laughed. "How can one god be three persons?"

Patrick smiled and bent over to pluck a shamrock from a nearby plant. Holding it up, he said, "This shamrock has three leaves and a stem. It is only complete the way it grows, yet although it has a stem and three leaves, it is only one shamrock. So it is with my God."

The assembly of nobles and warriors nodded. This they could understand, for the fields were filled with shamrocks.

"What does your God tell you to preach?" Lucetmal asked next.

"Love," Patrick said. "He teaches us to love our fellow men in a sacrificial way, just as He sacrificed Himself for those who were His spiritual children. You worship your gods merely out of fear. We worship the Lord because He has taught us to trust in His mercy, love, and grace. He teaches us that we are His creatures and that our souls will live forever with Him if we love and obey the Lord Jesus Christ. Someday," Patrick added, "the knowledge of the glory of my Lord and Savior Jesus Christ will fill the earth as the waters cover the seas. And men like you, Lucetmal, will be known to be evil."

The Druid was beside himself with rage. He screamed, "You are a wicked fool, Patrick," and then added, "and I curse your God too."

As soon as the words left the mouth of the Druid priest, he found that he could not speak any longer. All who were there saw Lucetmal clutch at his chest and saw his face contort with agony. They heard him moan, and then they watched him topple to the ground. He was dead.

Lochru threw himself on the lifeless body of his brother. He cried out, "O mighty Loegaire, this man has killed our beloved Lucetmal. I demand his death!"

The king arose. He was trembling from a mixture of anger and confusion. Loegaire was not used to being out of control in a given situation. "Seize him!" the enraged king sputtered.

The courageous bishop stood firm and called out, "May God arise and His enemies be scattered!" Darkness suddenly fell on the camp. Confused Druids and guards began to attack each other as frightened horses galloped off, smashing chariots in their path. A terrified king knelt before Patrick, though his eyes still flashed with anger. Loegaire cried out, "Call upon your God to bring this madness to an end," pleaded the desperate ruler.

Patrick prayed, and soon the sun began to appear out of the clouds once again. Every eye was locked upon the brave missionary, as he called upon the assembly to settle down and help him restore order. Then he turned to the king, who was shouting, "Where is Lochru?"

"He has had enough for one day," said the bishop boldly. "Lochru has gone to join the pagan gods that are hiding in your sacred woods, King." After Patrick spoke to the king, he gave his attention to the huge company of men and women who were now silent and frightened. "There is no need to fear," he told them. "My God is a just God. He commands only that you turn away from your false gods, love Him, and follow the teachings of His Holy Word. He has sent me here not to conquer your country, nor to overthrow your king, but merely to deliver you from the power of darkness and to show you the way to make peace with God. All I ask of you, King Loegaire, is permission to talk to your people about the claims of Christ upon their lives. Do I have your permission?"

"You do," Loegaire said, his voice trembling.

Queen Angas walked forward and knelt before Patrick. "You have showed yourself to be a brave and holy servant of the true God," she said earnestly. "The Druids represented nothing but evil and bondage. They have ruled over us all by fear and superstition. I for one wish to hear more of your God who is strong enough to love. I wish to have the kind of courageous faith and quiet confidence that you have shown us today. Will you show me the road to this faith?"

Patrick nodded. And then and there he preached the first of many sermons in the region of Tara.

COMPREHENSION QUESTIONS

1. Who was the High King of Tara during this time period?
2. Why did Patrick feel that he needed to confront Loegaire?
3. Who was Arin?
4. Who was the only Person that Patrick believed was worthy of glory?
5. Why was Lochru angry with Bishop Patrick?
6. Who did Patrick say created the heaven and earth?

WORDS TO KNOW

earnestly	contort
bondage	sacrilege
celebration	defy
confused	ignited

Victory Over the Druids

Patrick remained at the court of Loegaire for several months. The Queen became one of his first converts, and after he baptized her, she ordered a church to be built on the Hill of Slane. Shortly after the baptismal service, the Queen decided to send a special gift to the bishop which included gold and rare jewels. The servant who endeavored to deliver the gifts was not successful, however, for Patrick told the man to return the gift to the Queen with his thanks.

When the tired servant returned the unopened gifts to Queen Angas she was quite amazed. "Are you sure that Bishop Patrick knew that the gifts were for him?" asked the Queen.

"Yes, your highness, he knew very well that the gifts were for him personally," insisted the servant boy. "He wanted me to tell you not to be offended but that he could not accept gifts for the simple act of leading souls to Christ. The bishop suggested that perhaps you might want to donate some of the gifts to an orphanage that he is starting in a nearby village."

"Well, if that is what this man of God prefers, then so be it," said the stunned woman.

Simple actions from Patrick, such as the one just described, as well as the more celebrated victories against the Druids, earned him a reputation as a true man of God. Yet Ireland, dotted with scores of tiny, warring kingdoms and fanatical Druids, must be won step by step.

In light of the fact that Tara was the largest realm in Ireland, Patrick decided to visit every castle and village in the area he possibly could. As Patrick and his missionary team approached a castle, they would offer presents of fine linens or food to secure an audience with the local chieftain. Then they would tell the leader and his family about the wonderful news of salvation in Christ, His death on the cross and His resurrection from the dead. In many instances, the Lord used these meetings to enable Patrick to gain the liberty he needed to preach openly throughout a particular realm.

There was something about Patrick's exuberant faith and steadfast character that attracted these warlike chieftains. As months turned into years, Patrick and his followers traveled throughout the eastern portion of Ireland preaching, building churches, and making disciples. For five years, he and his band trod through forests and over countless hills to call the people to God. On many occasions, the bishop of Ireland would exhort his followers to "...fish well and diligently, as our Lord requires. Hence, we spread our nets so that a great multitude and throng might be caught for God."

At the end of five years of ceaseless toil, Patrick's team, which now included a new volunteer from Britain named Secundinus, came to a place called Domach. This area was ruled by Connal, the brother of Loegaire, who welcomed Patrick and his men.

"I have heard much about you, holy Patrick," he said.

"My brother Loegaire and his lovely queen have told me how you destroyed the power of the Druids. I am ready to believe in your God, Patrick. But if I said so publicly, my people would slay me."

"Why is that, Connal?" Patrick asked.

"Know this, Patrick," Connal responded. "The Druids are more powerful in my territory than in any other part of Ireland. For centuries, this has been the home of the idol that all the Druids worship. The idol is made of stone, covered with gold and silver bands, and it stands upon a hill not far from here at a place called Crom Cruach."

"I have heard of this pagan idol," Patrick said.

"Even those of us who are kings," Connal said sadly, "do not know of all the things that happen when the Druids sacrifice to this idol. We do know that once a year, when the Druids come here, young girls and our strongest boys disappear from the face of the earth. We are certain that they are sacrificed at Crom Cruach by the Druids. Do you wonder that my people fear the power of these men of darkness? As long as the idol stands, Patrick, you cannot preach in this part of Ireland, for the people would stone you."

Patrick began to pace slowly up and down as he repeated to himself, "As long as the idol stands." He quietly prayed for wisdom in regard to the removal of the giant idol at Crom Cruach. The next morning, Patrick, Secundinus, and Arin determined to take a first hand look at the Druid idol that was located on a nearby mountain.

After a long walk, these servants of Christ found themselves looking upon the huge idol. It looked every bit as large as Connal had said. It was shaped like a hideous monster, and blood stained the base of the idol. Four Druids stood before the idol in their white robes.

"Welcome, O stranger," one of them said to Patrick, casting an eye to see if the men had brought any children with them. "Do you come here to offer sacrifice? The great god at Crom Cruach desires a pleasing sacrifice such as a young boy."

"I have come to speak of another kind of sacrifice," Patrick said angrily.

"But the only way to please our god is by human sacrifice," the Druid said.

"Sacrifice to that ugly, useless piece of stone?" Patrick stormed. The Druid cried out sharply, and a dozen warriors whose tents were in a nearby field came running with their swords drawn.

"This man has defied our great spirit," the Druid cried. "Seize him!"

The warriors grabbed a hold of Patrick and took him as a prisoner. The Druid priest proceeded to inform Patrick's companions that they would never see their friend alive again unless they brought a gift of atonement to the altar at Crom Cruach. The gift or ransom was ten pieces of gold and a young boy or girl for their use.

"Go now you two foolish ones," said the Druid, "and

bring back your offerings to our god within five days or the prisoner dies."

Patrick nodded his head and told his men to leave for five days and then to return and see what God can do to a pagan idol. "Please go in peace my friends," Patrick added, "and cease not to pray for my faith to stand strong in this place of evil."

The followers of Patrick reluctantly made their way down the hill and back toward the castle of their friend Connal. All along the way, these men poured out fervent prayers for their imprisoned bishop. Upon reaching the castle, the men informed Connal of Patrick's captivity and the ransom terms that were established by the Druids.

"I'm not surprised," said Connal sadly. "If only Patrick would have listened to my warnings!"

As Connal and the followers of Patrick debated about the proper course of action, the Lord was already at work among the Druids. Each of the four pagan priests who held Patrick against his will suddenly became very sick. Within twelve hours from the time the bishop of Ireland was taken captive, a great sickness began to descend upon the Druid camp. The sickness began with a burning fever and a horrible headache then quickly developed into the loathsome disease known as boils. Large blisters began to appear all over the bodies of the Druid priests and their warrior servants.

For two long days, the pagan priests and their men suffered mightily. They tried in a desperate fashion to use their black magic to rid themselves of their sickness, but nothing helped. In fact, the more they cried unto their idols, the sicker they became. After the third night of utter misery, the Druids finally resolved to speak to their captive.

"Your God is the cause of all of our sickness, evil stranger," muttered the sickly Druid leader. "If you tell your God to remove His curse from our midst, we will let you go in safety."

"My God is greatly offended by your wicked stone idol and your evil sacrifices," said Patrick boldly. "If you and your men desire to avoid a miserable death, then you will need to sacrifice your stone idol. You must pull down and break apart this idol and never build it up again!"

"Never!" cried the Druid priest, but as he spoke his legs collapsed under him. He was dead. The remaining Druids watched as worms quickly devoured the servant of darkness.

It did not take long for one of the remaining Druids to speak up. "We now know that your God is indeed the

master over all gods and priests. Therefore, we will do as you ask and tear down our stone altar and destroy the image at Crom Cruach."

"Very well, then get to it before the patience of the living God runs out!" responded the sincere captive. "And remove these chains from my feet and arms this instant."

It took several minutes for the Druids and the warriors to pull down the heavy stone idol. After considerable effort, however, the huge stone image began to totter, and while the Druids watched with sad eyes, it fell and smashed into tiny pieces.

"May all the false idols ever built in this country go the same way!" Patrick cried. "And may the people of Ireland know that there is only one true God, Whose Son is Jesus."

As Patrick finished speaking, his missionary companions were approaching the crest of the hill. When they finally came within sight of Patrick and the smashed idol, they could hardly believe their eyes. They had expected to see their friend in a bad way, but instead, saw a great answer to prayer.

The bishop of Ireland gave a final warning to the Druid priests to abandon their work of idolatry and murder, then turned away and led his little group back to the castle. Connal and all of his court had already heard from the townspeople what had happened at Crom Cruach. As Patrick approached, Connal fell on his knees. "Teach us, O holy Patrick, the true path, and we shall follow it," he implored. "Tell us what to do to find peace with the Christian God."

"First of all, my friend, please get up from your knees," Patrick said simply. "We are all unworthy and sinful men who need to draw close to our Maker. As for the path of peace, you and your people must forsake your sinful ways that make God angry with you, and trust in the Lord Jesus Christ as Savior and King. He has already come to this earth as a sinless man and died on a cross to pay for the sins of all those who will trust in His gracious sacrifice. This same Christ also rose from the dead so He could demonstrate His power over death. Now He is alive forevermore with His Father in Heaven and has sent the Holy Spirit to be with us. Anyone who trusts in Jesus Christ will also obtain the gift of eternal life and will be able to serve God according to His Word."

"Please stay with us brother Patrick," pleaded Connal. "We have much to learn and need a faithful shepherd."

"I will stay dear friend," responded Saint Patrick. "God has many of his little lambs in this region and I must bring them into the fold of Christ Jesus."

For two years, Patrick remained with Connal and his people. Every week, representatives came from other parts of Ireland, pleading with Patrick to come and show their people the way to God. He promised that, if God permitted, he would in time visit their part of the country. The Lord Himself had begun to multiply the missionary efforts of Patrick by placing a great hunger in the Irish people to be delivered from the darkness and bondage of the Druid religion.

"I shall not be satisfied," said the bishop of Ireland solemnly, "until all of Ireland is delivered from pagan darkness and brought to the point of accepting the true God."

COMPREHENSION QUESTIONS

1. Why was Queen Angas amazed by the response of Patrick to her gift?
2. Why were the warlike chieftains attracted to Patrick?
3. Who or what was Crom Cruach?
4. What happened to the four Druid priests who took Patrick captive?
5. How long did Patrick stay with Connal and his people?
6. How did God multiply the missionary efforts of Saint Patrick?

WORDS TO KNOW

exuberant	solemn
donate	totter
stunned	atonement
celebrated	ransom

CHAPTER 17

The Gospel Seed Grows

The story of how the great idol had fallen was soon heard all over Ireland, and the people who had lived in fear of the Druids for centuries now laughed at them. The Irish people finally began to realize that the Druids were evil men who only wanted power for themselves.

When Patrick moved into the western portions of Ireland, the people flocked to see the saintly man who dared to challenge the powers of darkness. Everywhere the bishop went, he preached the simple message of salvation in Christ and baptized those who repented from their sins and accepted the God of the Bible. Saint Patrick also made a point of leaving the people with some portion of Scripture and, whenever possible, a building for worship.

While Patrick was working among the people, Loegaire, the mightiest of the Irish kings, suddenly died. After his death, his brother Connal was made king. The first thing the new king did was to banish all Druids from his court. He also sent messengers all over Ireland with an order that Christian missionaries were to be allowed to preach and build churches.

The new king also gave Patrick a chariot drawn by horses to enable the aging missionary to travel more swiftly around the Irish countryside. This transportation permitted Patrick to visit many of the churches he had started in the northern and eastern parts of Ireland. It also helped him reach out to new areas such as the western region of Ireland.

During one of Patrick's first trips to the western portion of Ireland, he decided to go to the Croagh mountain range which is located along the restless Atlantic Ocean, for prayer and contemplation. This wise missionary understood that if he was going to have the necessary power to overcome the hosts of hell in western Ireland, he would first need to pray. For this reason, he is said to have spent forty days and forty nights on this mountain range wrestling with God in prayer and fasting.

As soon as Patrick was spiritually prepared, he came down from the mountains and began to minister to the needs of lost souls. More months passed as the bishop of Ireland tramped down the roads and forded the rivers of the green isle in an effort to see children and adults "reborn in God."

By the year 447, within fifteen years of Patrick's landing on the east coast of the island, a large part of Ireland had been evangelized and hundreds of churches had been planted. The growth of Christian communities in Ireland had taken place so rapidly that it soon became clear to Patrick that a synod needed to be formed to unite the churches. Without such an ecclesiastical organization, Patrick feared that the churches in Ireland would not mature properly or be well coordinated.

For this reason, Patrick and other church leaders selected the city of Armagh to be used as a type of headquarters for the Christian church in Ireland. Bishop Patrick was selected as the leader of the Synod at Armagh and was directed to travel there for the purpose of establishing a permanent base of operations and church somewhere in the area.

As was his custom, Patrick decided that as soon as he reached Armagh, he would visit the local ruler and seek to obtain his blessing on the work he planned to do. Upon arriving in the city, the bishop of Ireland went directly to King Daire of Armagh to request a hilltop site on which to build a church. The ruler was unwilling to grant Patrick a choice hilltop site for his building project, however, and instead offered him a spot on lower ground. Patrick humbly accepted the offer and began to make preparations to build.

Several days later, in an effort to elevate himself in the eyes of the people, Daire sent Patrick a valuable three-gallon bronze pot imported from Gaul. "Thanks be to God," the missionary said upon receipt of the pot. Daire became enraged, however, when he heard of Patrick's response.

"Stupid man! Doesn't he have any more grateful words for my gift than 'thanks be to God?'" said the proud king as he turned to his servant. "If this is the way I am to be treated," muttered the ruler, "then go to this foolish preacher and demand that he return the pot."

When Daire's servant came before Patrick to collect the pot, all the bishop would say was "thanks be to God, take it away." King Daire was so astonished by the missionary's humble reply that he came out to the construction site to meet with him personally.

As the king talked at length with the bishop of Ireland, he began to admire the inner strength and determination of this servant of Christ. "This place is not good enough for your church, holy man," bellowed Daire. "You wanted the Ridge of the Willows in the first pace. I demand that you take this hilltop site for your God!"

"If you wish to let us build on a better site, then we will honor your desire, good King," said the grateful bishop.

This unusual confrontation between the king of Armagh and Bishop Patrick was of tremendous benefit to the Christian church for many years. The leaders of the Christian church in Ireland often met in Armagh to discuss the needs of the people of God. As they met together, they could rely upon the help and protection of the local king. This same situation was also becoming more and more commonplace throughout Ireland as local kings began to abandon their allegiance to the Druid religion in favor of Christianity.

As the church in Armagh continued to grow, one of Patrick's faithful ministers came up to him with a suggestion. "Dear Brother Patrick," he said, "you once told me that to convert the people we should first have to convert the kings. We have, by God's grace, converted many rulers. The power of the Druids is broken. Now let us think of teaching the children."

"Excellent idea, old friend," said Patrick. "I will speak to the council about this matter of church schools in the near future."

Bishop Patrick was able to encourage his fellow council members to begin building church schools throughout the country.

The bishop of Ireland was burdened to see Christian schools established in Ireland, in part because he himself was deprived of a good education when he was a boy. Although it took many years, a number of Christian schools and universities were eventually built throughout the land.

In his speedy chariot, Patrick also went far to the west, to the land called Connaught, a place of lakes and gentle hills. Here the valleys teamed with skylarks, and birds seemed to be singing their best when Patrick arrived. He talked with the people of Connaught, built churches, and made many disciples.

The people loved him so much that they tried to worship him as a god. They crowded close to touch his robe and held up their babies for him to look upon.

"I am only a humble servant of God," he would tell them. "There is only one God and we must worship Him alone. I have come to bring you His Word and I beg you to build your lives around the teachings of the Holy Scripture."

When Patrick left Connaught, two of his ministers remained there to disciple the people in the Scriptures and supervise the building of houses of worship.

As the bishop of Ireland moved on to the city of Donegal in northwestern Ireland he called upon the king of this territory to present him with the message of Christ.

This king had heard of Patrick and of the amazing feats he had performed. When the king questioned Patrick about the miraculous deeds he had done, the humble bishop told him that he himself could not perform a miracle.

"Only Almighty God can do that," he would say. "I am merely the instrument He uses to accomplish His will on earth."

The king of Donegal granted Patrick the liberty to talk to the people, and as they listened to his messages of salvation and brotherly love, many of them gradually came to faith in God. Nobles and peasants alike could recognize that the humble bishop wanted no power for himself. He was merely trying to help people find peace with God through a relationship with the Lord Jesus Christ. He told everyone who would listen about the glories that awaited God's people in Heaven, and urged them to stop fighting among themselves. As the common people listened, they too began to believe. A world at peace was something they had never known. They were looking forward to a pleasant change from the constant warfare between families and rulers. In time, the message of peace that was preached by Patrick was embraced by many souls in Ireland.

After four years of traveling, Patrick turned his chariot toward the land of Dichu. As he entered this region, it brought back many memories of his first weeks as a missionary in Ireland. Patrick noticed a new building on the top of the very hill where Dunbar had stood years before and unleashed his dogs at his supposed enemies. He decided to visit this new building to see if his old friend Kent was still at this location after so long a period.

No sooner had Patrick reached the front door of the new building than a middle-aged man appeared at the door.

As soon as the two men set eyes on each other, they began to smile. The two seasoned preachers, Kent and Patrick, began to embrace.

"From what I have heard Bishop Patrick, you seldom slow down to stop anywhere," said Kent with a lighthearted sigh. "Now, however, you simply must stay in one place for awhile. This is your home from now on."

The men shook hands once again as Kent began to show him through the school and new house. "You have traveled far, and you must be tired, Brother," asserted Kent. "Henceforth, remain here and let the people come to you for a change. I have made the church building larger in recent years and it will hold all those who wish to hear you preach."

"But will they come all the way up here?" questioned the bishop.

"Patrick," Kent said with feeling, "perhaps you have been too busy to know what you have done. When you visit a place like Munster, you talk to the people and build a church. Then you leave one of your ministers in charge and start out for some other place. You do not seem to realize that the seeds of faith that you have planted have been used by God the Holy Spirit to grow a mighty church. The people of God hold your work in the highest regard, as do I."

After a few moments of silence, Kent added, "The story of how you are supposed to have driven the snakes from the country is being told all over Ireland. You are indeed the best known leader in the land."

"Snakes?" Patrick asked puzzled. "Oh yes, I remember. There was a place in Munster the Druids called the Hill of Snakes. They held their evil sacrifices on this hill and told the people that anyone who went to the hill would be killed by the bite of a snake. I preached from that hill and built a church there, and told the people that the snakes would not bother them. You and I know, Kent, that snakes seldom attack people unless the people bother them first. And because I said that, they think I drove the snakes out of Munster?"

"They say you drove the snakes out of Ireland," Kent corrected him with a smile. "It is a story they will be telling a thousand years from now. Oh, they tell all sorts of stories about you, and these will all be believed."

Patrick was silent for a moment. Then he said, very plainly, "I only want to be remembered as the man who brought the Word of God to a pagan people, and helped them to know the true faith."

"You will be known as the one who brought a whole savage country to God," Kent said with conviction.

The two brothers in Christ finished their conversation and took a short break for a meal. After the meal was over, Patrick confessed that he was tired of the almost constant burden of traveling from place to place. He proceeded to inform his host that he would settle down for a few months in his home and preach to all who would come.

Just as Kent had predicted, the next few Sundays saw the first Christian church in Ireland filled with hundreds of people who came to hear Patrick preach. He had the pleasure of baptizing many converts and training a number of men for the mission field during the first year he was reunited with Kent's congregation.

Not all of the issues that Kent and Patrick faced were as pleasant as baptisms and weddings. One spring afternoon, Kent received a letter from the bishop of Armagh informing him that thousands of new converts were being murdered or kidnapped in the north of Ireland by raiders under the control of a British king named Coroticus.

As soon as Kent finished reading the letter from Armagh, he went directly to Patrick's private study to share the bad news.

"Bishop," said Kent in a sober voice, "I have a serious issue to speak with you about. Can we talk?"

"Certainly," said Patrick as he closed the book he was reading. "I suggest, however, that we pray together for a time before we begin to wrestle with this matter. As you well know, Brother Kent, God gives wisdom to His servants only when they ask for it."

COMPREHENSION QUESTIONS

1. How did Patrick's work at Crom Cruach free the Irish from Druid bondage?
2. Why did Patrick decide to visit the Croagh mountains?
3. What city was selected as the headquarters of the Irish church?
4. What gift did King Daire initially give to Patrick?
5. Why was Patrick burdened to help local churches build schools?
6. What bad news did Kent intend on sharing with Bishop Patrick?

WORDS TO KNOW

predicted	allegiance
reunited	forded
supervise	tramped
confrontation	evangelize

CHAPTER 18

The Lost Sheep

Brother Kent handed the letter over to his old friend, Patrick, as the two men sat in front of a large fire place. It took a minute or two for Patrick to read the lengthy letter from the bishop of Armagh. When he had finished reading, he rose to his feet and looked deeply saddened. Finally, after pacing the floor for a period, he told his companion, "I am deeply grieved to hear that Irish Christians are being murdered by wicked men. But at least these saints are dying a martyr's death and will immediately enjoy their rewards in heaven. As for the others who have been kidnapped and enslaved, my heart is grieved beyond measure for I know how miserable a slave's life can be. I think the young women who are taken captive and sold are the most miserable by far."

"You are undoubtedly right, dear Bishop. But the question still remains as to what we should do to aid our persecuted brethren and to stop the British slave raiders," stated Kent plainly. "Do you know this king from the west coast of Britain?"

"I have never heard of the ruler named Coroticus," responded Patrick. "My work in Ireland these many years has caused me to lose touch with affairs in Britain. I still have a few contacts among the bishops in Britain, perhaps I could contact them to gain their advice on the best course of action."

"As you wish, Bishop," said Kent simply.

The following day, the bishop of Ireland wrote to various church leaders in Britain who eventually responded to his plea for guidance. The general opinion was that Patrick should send a delegation of Irish church leaders to the court of Coroticus in hopes of being able to ransom the captives that he held. As a result of this counsel, Patrick directed the Synod leaders in Armagh to appoint a small group of bishops to travel to western Britain for the purpose of negotiating with King Coroticus.

The following month, several Irish bishops sailed to Britain to confront the wayward king, but when they arrived at the king's residence, they were simply laughed out of his presence. The bishops were not even permitted to speak with the proud British king who ordered them to be put on the next ship bound for Ireland.

It did not take long for the news regarding this failed journey to reach the ears of Bishop Patrick. Upon receiving the bad news, the patience of Patrick began to give way to righteous anger. After a brief season of prayer, the angry bishop determined to prepare a lengthy letter to the tyrant Coroticus which would condemn his actions and threaten him with excommunication. The letter Patrick sent was also intended to openly condemn the ungodly practice of kidnapping people for the purpose of selling them as slaves. Bishop Patrick hoped that this letter would motivate church leaders in Britain to put pressure on Coroticus to release his captive slaves.

Patrick's now famous letter to Coroticus became a call to the church in Britain to stop ignoring the plight of persecuted Christians who were being "eaten up by raving wolves as if they were bread." Patrick used all of his powers of persuasion to tell his British brothers how they ought to treat slave raiders and the rulers who support them. He wrote, "...I beseech you earnestly, it is not right to pay taxes to such men nor to take food and drink in their company, nor is it right to accept their alms, until they by doing strict penance with shedding of tears, make amends before God, and free the servants of God and the baptized handmaids of Christ for whom he was crucified and died."

The bishop of Ireland passionately hoped that his letter would prick the consciences of the church leaders in Britain to unite and excommunicate Coroticus. Such an action, Patrick believed, would eventually create such an extensive wall of social isolation around the rebellious ruler that he would lose his resolve to keep the Irish captives. In many respects, Patrick was like Moses of old who told a stubborn ruler to "let my people go!"

As the months passed by, Patrick continued to monitor the crisis in the north of Ireland and gave special encouragement to the church leaders in this region. Eventually, it became clear that Patrick's efforts to secure the release of his brothers and sisters in Britain would meet with only limited success. This was due in part to the fact that many church leaders in Britain were not fully persuaded that Irish Christians were truly a part of the church.

At one point in Patrick's correspondence with leaders in Britain, he asked as he cried out in his spiritual pain, "Is it a shameful thing that we have been born in Ireland? Can it be," he added, "that you do not believe that we have received one baptism, or that we have one God and Father?" As is often the case throughout church history, the people of God lose many blessings when they refuse to bear each other's burdens and stand with fellow believers in a unified manner.

Although Bishop Patrick had but limited success in his efforts to relieve the suffering of Christian slaves in Britain, this entire episode stands as a mighty testimony to the greatness of the former slave from Bannavem. Patrick was very possibly the most eloquent human being in the history of the world to speak out openly and clearly against ungodly systems of slavery. As has often been said, "Some goals are so excellent that it is even glorious to fail." In the case of Patrick and his efforts to rescue his "lost sheep," this saying certainly rings true.

Comprehension Questions

1. Where did King Coroticus live?
2. Why did Patrick send a delegation of bishops to Britain?
3. Why did Patrick write a letter to church leaders in Britain?
4. Did Patrick have success in getting the slaves set free?
5. Were the church leaders in Britain totally united with their brethren in Ireland?
6. Should success always be the measure of good?

Words to Know

excommunication	alms
conscience	wayward
beseech	kidnapped
handmaid	negotiate

CHAPTER 19

Patrick Finishes His Race

As the year 460 unfolded, Patrick could scarcely believe that he had been serving the Lord in Ireland for almost thirty years. In spite of numerous difficulties and several imprisonments, the bishop of Ireland continued to serve the needs of the church faithfully and tirelessly.

At this point in Patrick's ministry, he finally took time out of his busy schedule to make a record of his experiences as a child of God from youth to old age. He wrote a lengthy summary of his life under the title of *The Confession of Patrick*. A great deal of what we know about Bishop Patrick and his life comes down to us through this written record.

It is in the *Confession*, and his lengthy letter to Coroticus, that Patrick himself lets us know what he was thinking and experiencing during the last few years of his life. The bishop of Ireland tells us that he was immensely grateful to God for giving him the privilege of helping to transform a pagan land of darkness into a blessed land filled with Christian light. He also acknowledges the gracious way in which God worked through him. Patrick states, "...It was not my grace, but God, victorious in me, who resisted all opposition when I came to the people of Ireland to preach the gospel and to suffer insults from unbelievers. If I should be worthy, I am ready to give even my life most willingly for His Name. I am bound by the Spirit who witnesses to me. Christ the Lord told me to come here and stay with the Irish for the rest of my life, if He so wills, and He will guard me from every evil way that I might not sin before Him."

As one studies the writings of Patrick, it is very clear that he perceived his call to Ireland as a lifelong commitment. He remained constant in his mission to convert the whole of Ireland. Never once did he take the time for a trip home or a lengthy vacation. His joy came through his service to the lost sheep of Ireland—and serve he did!

Toward the end of Patrick's life, we find him visiting churches, baptizing new converts, training new ministers, encouraging those who are operating schools or orphanages, and providing for the needs of the poor. In other words, Bishop Patrick continued to

do the very things that he had been doing ever since he landed in Ireland. He continued steadfast and unmovable.

As any reader might expect, Patrick never left his beloved Ireland. He died on March 17, 461, in the midst of his work and with a heart full of gratitude to Almighty God. The land which once enslaved him, he had set free by the grace of the Lord Jesus Christ. Saint Patrick's body was buried in the churchyard of the ancient Cathedral of Down. His gravestone in Downpatrick simply reads PATRIC.

The example that Patrick set inspired an entire generation to live for Christ. Not since the days of the Apostle Paul had any Christian missionary been as influential or successful in the work of discipling nations as Patrick had been. It is also not surprising to find that one hundred years after Patrick's death in 461, the church in Ireland possessed such a vigorous faith that it was aggressively sending out mission-

aries to countries such as Scotland, England, France, and
Germany. The once pagan nation would soon be known as
the "Isle of Saints." Even today, the people of Ireland are
generally considered to be brave, steadfast, and generous.

More than any other human being, Bishop Patrick
understood that it was God's presence and power in his
life that kept him safe and fruitful in his missionary work.

The bishop of Ireland, towards the later portion of
his life, wrote a wonderful prayer that testified to the fact
that the Lord was the strength of his life. This prayer is
often called "Saint Patrick's Breastplate." From the depths
of a grateful soul, Patrick penned these beautiful thoughts:

I arise today
Through a mighty strength, the invocation of the Trinity,
Through belief in the threeness,
Through confession of the oneness
Of the Creator of Creation.

I arise today
Through the strength of Christ's birth with his baptism,
Through the strength of his crucifixion with his burial,
Through the strength of his resurrection with his ascension,
Through the strength of his descent for the judgment of Doom.

...I arise today Through God's strength to pilot me:
God's might to uphold me,
God's wisdom to guide me,
God's eye to look before me,
God's ear to hear me,
God's word to speak for me,
God's hand to guard me,

God's way to lie before me,
God's host to save me,
From snares of devils,
From temptations of vices,
From everyone who shall wish me ill,
Afar and anear,
Alone and in multitude.

...Christ to shield me today
Against poison, against burning,
Against drowning, against wounding,
So that there may come to me abundance of reward.
Christ with me, Christ before me, Christ behind me,
Christ in me, Christ beneath me, Christ above me,
Christ on my right, Christ on my left,
Christ when I lie down, Christ when I sit down, Christ when I rise,
Christ in the heart of every man who thinks of me,
Christ in the mouth of everyone who speaks of me,
Christ in every eye that sees me,
Christ in every ear that hears me.

I arise today
Through a mighty strength, the invocation of the Trinity.
Through belief in the threeness,
Through confession of the oneness,
Of the Creator of Creation.

Bishop Patrick overcame numerous problems during his years of service simply because he understood that he was never alone—that God was his constant companion. The good news for any Christian living in the twenty-first century is that the same God who shepherded Saint Patrick is ready and able to empower people with child-like faith today to pull down the strongholds of Satan.

There is much myth and legend associated with the life of Patrick, Bishop of Ireland. Regardless of the myths, however, we can be certain that he was a humble missionary who was utterly devoted to preaching the simple message of the gospel of Christ. Patrick never considered himself as any type of super "saint." This brave Christian, like all true servants of Christ, are called to be "saints" solely on account of their redemption by God. At no time did Patrick ever seek any title or recognition from any church councils or popes in Rome. His whole priority in life was to seek to be approved by Christ as a faithful workman in the independent Celtic church of Ireland. Snakes, leprechauns, and magic charms were distant from him. Saint Patrick believed the Bible to be supreme in all matters of faith and life. No matter what the legends about him may say, the truth is that Patrick found the strength and wisdom to disciple the nation of Ireland by the Spirit of God and the Word of God.

Just as in Patrick's day, any child of God who wishes to overcome the world must be willing to follow the call of Christ to pick up in faith the cross of love and service and follow Him. Patrick was indeed a truly great man of God. His example of perseverance under tremendous pressure, his unswerving faith in God's call upon his life, and his personal piety, all join together to inspire believers today to follow after Christ and to make Him known to the nations.

COMPREHENSION QUESTIONS

1. How long had Patrick served Christ in Ireland by the year 460?
2. What did Patrick write about in his *Confession*?
3. Who did Patrick credit for transforming Ireland into a Christian nation?
4. How many lengthy vacations did Patrick take as a missionary?
5. In what way was Saint Patrick steadfast and unmovable?
6. Where was Patrick's body buried?

WORDS TO KNOW

influential	insult
orphanage	ascension
invocation	snare
vigorous	descent

BIBLIOGRAPHY

Bury, J. B. *The Life of St. Patrick and His Place in History.* London, 1905.

Cahill, Thomas. *How the Irish Saved Civilization.* New York: Doubleday, 1995.

Edman, V. Raymond. *The Light In Dark Ages.* Illinois: Van Kampen Press, 1949.

Galli, Mark, ed. "How the Irish Were Saved." *Christian History,* November 1998.

Gray, Andrew. *The Origin and Early History of Christianity in Britain.* 1897. California: Artisan Sales Press, 1991 reprint.

Hanson, R.P.C. *St. Patrick: His Origins and Career.* Oxford, 1968.

Hood, A.B.E. *St. Patrick: His Writings and Muirchu's Life.* London: Chichester, 1978.

Mac Neill, Eoin. *St. Patrick the Apostle of Ireland.* London, 1934.

Meyer, Kuno. *Selections from Ancient Irish Poetry.* London, 1911.

Reynolds, Quentin. *The Life of Saint Patrick.* New York: Random House, 1955.

Stokes, Whitley. *The Tripartie Life of St. Patrick.* London, 1887.